WHAT IS
GOD?

Answering the World's
Most Important Question
(with help from Thomas Aquinas)

KEVIN VOST, PSY.D.

Catholic
Answers
Press

Published by Catholic Answers, Inc.
2020 Gillespie Way
El Cajon, California 92020
1-888-291-8000 orders
619-387-0042 fax
catholic.com

Printed in the United States of America

Cover design by Shane Riter
Interior design by Claudine Mansour Design

978-1-68357-294-7
978-1-68357-295-4 Kindle
978-1-68357-296-1 ePub

To Aleyna Belle Vost

"Grandchildren are the crown of the aged."

Proverbs 17:6

CONTENTS

ACKNOWLEDGMENTS

Many thanks to Todd Aglialoro, who edited my first, second, third, fifth, sixth, and ninth books, and gave the green light to number twenty-two and to this one, number twenty-four. Thanks, too, to Drew Belsky. He took over from there, straightened my circuitous route, and deftly guided this book across the finish line. Thanks to all at Catholic Answers Press involved in bringing this Thomistic tome to print. Thanks to Kathy Ann Vost for keeping our house in order while enduring my ceaseless chatter about all things Thomistic. Of course, were it not for St. Thomas Aquinas, there would be no *What Is God?* And without the God he wrote about, there would be nothing at all.

WHAT IS THE WORLD'S GREATEST QUESTION?

People of all cultures, throughout all climes and all times, have pondered this fundamental question. Is God a friendly (but sometimes grumpy) bearded grandpa in the sky? Is God an impersonal force running through the universe? Is each one of us God in some way, if only we would wake up and realize it? Did humans make God? Is God a figment of the imagination?

If we speak broadly of God in the singular or of gods in the plural, as designating some sort of *divinity*, an entity or entities *super*-natural in the sense that a god's knowledge and powers far transcend those of nature and humanity and work in some way to control human destiny and the entire universe, we will see that peoples throughout time have come up with all sorts of tentative answers (which they may or may not have seen as tentative).

We might consider the beliefs regarding multiple gods, embraced by peoples as diverse as the Hindus in India and many ancient Egyptians, Greeks, Romans, Germanic and Nordic peoples, and others. These pantheons or families of gods differed significantly, both within and among various cultures' religions and mythologies.

We see remnants of their influence even in our time. Look up to the heavens on a dark, clear night and you will see the namesakes of the Roman god of war, Mars (Ares for the Greeks); the Roman goddess of love, Venus (Aphrodite); and even the Roman king of the gods, Jupiter (Zeus), along with the moon (Luna for the Romans). And of course you can look down at your feet to see Mother Earth (a primordial deity called Gaea for the Greeks).

Look at your space-age electronic calendar, and if you happen to be reading this on a Wednesday (as I am writing it), you are reading (and I am writing) on Woden's Day, named for Odin, the chief of the old Germanic gods. The old Norse mythology also has its say on Thursday (for Thor, the god of thunder) and Friday (for Frigga, Odin's wife).

We know that some ancient peoples also spoke not of gods in the plural, but of God in the singular. Whereas the ancient Egyptians believed in a variety of gods, often combining human and animal forms, the pharaoh Akhenaton of the fourteenth century B.C. worshipped one god: the sun-god Aten (and the pharaoh apparently claimed he was the only man who knew Aten personally).

The worship of Aten alone seems to have perished along with Akhenaton. But soon after, the ancient Jewish people, primarily through Moses, put true monotheism on the theological map, as it was proclaimed to them, they alleged, by none other than God himself! Indeed, the first of ten commandments God gave Moses was as follows: "I am the Lord your God. You shall have no other gods before me" (Exod. 20:2-3).

Some ancient Greek and Roman philosophers questioned the reality of their pantheon as described in the works of Hesiod, Homer, Virgil, and others. They strove to answer our question through human reason alone. Aristotle, for example, reasoned his way to a *Prime Mover* or *Unmoved Mover* who set the universe and humanity in motion, and this being he called God.

Epicurus and philosophers of his school took the position that gods existed, but they were too busy going about their divine business to care much or get involved in our merely human affairs. Those of the Atomist school, most notably Democritus and Leucippus, denied the existence of gods. They saw all reality as composed of atoms moving about according to chance, leaving no room for the soul or for spiritual beings. (Sounds a bit like many in our time, no?)

Reason led many Stoic philosophers to a belief in some kind of a single God. In debating with himself whether Atomists or theists were correct about the nature of God and reality, Roman emperor Marcus Aurelius posited the choice as "providence or atoms" and noted that although it is hard to be sure, he would choose to believe in God's providence over mere atoms.[1]

Aided by reason, but lacking in the divine revelation claimed by the Jews and Christians, the Stoics had varied conceptions of God that captured pieces and parts, we might say, of the truths of his nature. Various Stoics had vague and sometimes conflicting understandings of God as the shaper of the cosmos or universe (though not its creator), as the "breath" or "soul" of the universe, or as the universe or nature itself. Some held a *pantheistic* view—that everything is God, or a part of God.

Others, especially Seneca and Epictetus, did speak of God at times as a personal, father-like figure interested in our existence. Seneca wrote to his friend Lucilius, "God is near you, he is within you. This is what I mean, Lucilius: a holy spirit dwells within us, one who marks our good and bad deeds, and is our guardian."[2] Epictetus wrote, so poignantly,

> What else can I do, a lame old man, but sing hymns to God? If then I were a nightingale, I would do the nightingale's part; if I were a swan, I would do as a swan. But now I am a rational creature, and I ought to praise God: this is my work; I do it, nor will I desert my post, so long as I am allowed to keep it: and I exhort you to join in this same song.[3]

In the first century after the birth of Christ, Christians claimed, based on divine revelation, that the same *one* God who spoke to Moses was, in a mysterious way, also *three*: one in *substance*, but three in the *persons* of the Father, the Son, and the Holy Spirit. Further, the Son had become incarnate on earth in the God-man Jesus Christ. As the centuries went by, Christian philosophers and theologians also marshaled human reason to clarify and defend the existence of God.

One of the more interesting philosophical answers to our question, "What is God?", was proffered by St. Anselm of Canterbury of the eleventh and twelfth centuries: "By definition, God is a being of which nothing greater can be imagined." As one more century rolled by, more nuanced and powerful answers arose (as we will see), but not all were convinced.

With the rise of the *Age of Reason* or *Enlightenment* of

the sixteenth and seventeenth centuries, many prominent Western thinkers, among them the Frenchmen Voltaire and Diderot, cast serious doubt upon God's existence, at least as explained by Catholic teachings. The Enlightenment also gave strength to *deistic* views—the idea that reason can lead us to an impersonal God who created the universe but does not intervene in human affairs (sort of a monotheistic version of the views of some Epicureans). Deism was embraced by prominent figures in America, like Thomas Paine and some of the Founding Fathers of the United States.

Spurred by Darwin's writings about evolution, which seemed to cast doubt on man's special creation through the power of God (and in God's image and likeness), some prominent and outspoken philosophers of the nineteenth and twentieth centuries would express *atheistic* views. The German Friedrich Nietzsche, for example, declared that God is dead. He wrote with irreverent humor that when God proclaimed before an assembly of gods that he was the only god, they all died laughing. English philosopher Bertrand Russell launched more serious moral arguments against God's existence. He also, like Nietzsche, produced detailed critiques of Christian morality.

Our current day has given rise to a group of *new atheists*, some of them very outspoken, not merely in arguing that those who believe in God are mistaken, but in arguing that promotion of theistic views to children amounts to child abuse. Some of them also strive to remove any mention of God from the public square. Some answer our question, "What is God?", by calling belief in God a "delusion" and equating the rationality of belief in God with belief in elves or "the flying spaghetti monster."

So, after a whirlwind tour, we can see that there have

been a great many answers to our greatest of questions, many of which directly contradict many others. So how are we to make heads or tails out of all of this? Don't people usually grow up to believe whatever their parents or others in their culture happen to believe? Is any of these answers in the affirmative any better than the others? Why Jesus and not Apollo or Thor? We might cry out, "Lord help us!" . . . if we believe in God.

Well, I aver that God has already helped us, in a great many ways, to know important things about him well beyond the fact that he exists. Certainly, the greatest help God ever provided through *revelation* came in the birth of his Son on earth over 2,000 years ago. Perhaps the greatest help he provided through the use of human *reason* came with the birth of a fully human boy almost 800 years ago. It is to this boy's story we will turn next, dropping in at about the tender age of five.

"What is God? What is God? What is God?"

So asked the intellectually precious and religiously minded five-year-old, time and time again, to the poor Benedictine monks of Monte Cassino in Italy. The stories go that even as an infant, he had evidenced a thirst for knowledge. One day, when his mother, Theodora (whose name means "gift of God"), took him to the baths of Naples, he grabbed a piece of paper and refused to let go, bawling when it was taken from him. His mother found that the Hail Mary was written on it, and, in the interest of peace and quiet, she let him take it with him to the bath. The early biographer William of Tocco reported that after that, the only sure way to keep the young boy from crying was to give him something written on a piece of paper.*

Our precocious young lad, Thomas Aquinas (c. 1225–March 7, 1274), was the seventh child of an Italian lord and a relative of the imperial family. His mother and his father, Landulf, had plans for Thomas to one day become the abbot of the famous Benedictine monastery of Monte Cassino. Indeed, that was why he was taken there for training around the age of five, where he proceeded to pester the monks by posing again and again the most important of all human questions. We don't know for sure how the monks answered young Thomas, but we do know that, in a sense, Thomas devoted his powerful intellect and indominable will through the rest of his life to providing us with the best possible answers.

What is in this book?

This book contains Thomas's answers about God as provided in the masterwork of his voluminous writings, the over-3,000-page, over 1.5-million-word *Summa Theologica* (*ST*, or *Summa Theologiae*, as some scholars prefer). In brief, Thomas's great summary of theology contains thirty-eight treatises, each in itself a full-scale book by modern standards. The three major "parts" are devoted to God, man, and Christ, respectively, and are interrelated in an overarching *exitus-reditus* (out from God, back to God) theme.

---

* Simon Tugwell, O.P., has astutely observed, "His taste for books apparently antedated his ability to read!" Simon Tugwell, *Albert and Thomas: Selected Writings* (New York: Paulist Press, 1988), 202.

From God flows all creation, including man, who is made in his image and likeness. This is the stuff of Part I. Part II (subdivided into two parts of its own—I-II, "the first part of the second part," and II-II, "the second part of the second part") focuses on man's return to God through an examination of moral living, virtue, and God's gifts and graces. Part III completes man's return to God via Christ and his Church. After all, Christ told us, "I am the alpha and the omega, the first and the last, the beginning and the end" (Rev. 22:13), and "Before Abraham was, I am" (John 8:58). Further, as Thomas put it, Christ is both the *way* and the *destination*. In this sense, the *Summa Theologica* mirrors the structure of God's great plan for the universe.

The *Summa* is further structured in a formal way, being divided into a number of questions, 611 in all, including the "Supplement," ninety-nine questions compiled from Thomas's other writings after he died before his great *Summa* was finished.

Now, each of those 611 *questions* is divided into a series of *articles*, which examine topics that flesh out understanding of each general question. A simple, shorthand method of helping us pin down specific contents in the *Summa* is to identify the *part*, *question*, and *article* in which what we're looking for is found. Here's an example: *ST*, I, Q. 25, a. 4. Question 25 of the first part is labeled "The Power of God." It comprises six articles that examine God's omnipotence from multiple angles. Articles are labeled in the form of questions. The fourth one, for example, reads, "Whether God Can Make the Past Not to Have Been?" (We'll find the answer in the fourth section of our chapter 25.)

Further, every article begins with a series of numbered

objections—often three, but sometimes well over a dozen. These are arguments contrary to Thomas's conclusions, and they usually include citations from biblical or other sources. Thomas then states, "On the contrary," and provides a paragraph or so in which he typically includes a quotation in support of his conclusion. Next, he states, "I answer that . . ." and proceeds to give his own well reasoned and referenced conclusions. Not finished yet, he *replies* to each one of the objections presented at the start, typically revealing how the objections misconstrue the scriptural, patristic, or philosophical passages on which they're based. Talk about thorough!

In this book we will examine all of the first twenty-six questions and 157 articles of the *Summa Theologica*, for these most explicitly answer our question: "What is God?" Though I will modernize, summarize, and adapt their wording somewhat, each of our chapters corresponds to each of Thomas's questions, and each section heading within each chapter corresponds to one of his articles, all of this in the original order.

What kinds of issues will we examine? We'll start with preliminary questions like these:

- What is *theology*, or the study of God?

- Is God's existence self-evident to us?

- Can God's existence be proven through reason?

- How can evil exist in a world created by a God who's all-powerful and all-good?

- What are five ways to prove God's existence?

That will take us up to Thomas's Question (and our chapter) 3. For the remainder of our chapters, we will dig deep by addressing specific questions such as these:

- As complex as the universe is, would not God have to be infinitely more complex?

- What are God's five "primordial entitative attributes"?

- What are God's three "secondary entitative attributes"?

- Why is it impossible for there to be more than one God?

- Who made God?

- Could God create a boulder so heavy that even he cannot lift it?

- How can God be all-knowing and all-powerful? (If he knows what he's going to do tomorrow, how can he have the power to do something different?)

- Could God make the past not to have been? (I mentioned this one before. Hang in there for chapter 25.)

- How can God be both completely just and completely merciful?

- Is God really love?

- Is God happy?

Why are such questions so vitally important today?

Questions such as these, and so many more, are extremely important, not only for the fascination and edification of those who already love God, but because they can serve as a bridge to God for those who reject faith and swear to be guided only by science or reason. This I know both from reading and from personal experience.

Though raised Catholic, in my late teens I was lured into a quarter of a century of atheism through reading the arguments of atheistic and agnostic philosophers like Friedrich Nietzsche, Bertrand Russell, and Ayn Rand, as well as the psychologist Albert Ellis. (I'm too old to have been influenced by the current crop of new atheists, who, I might opine, are not quite up to the old standard.) These people were truly brilliant in some of their areas of expertise: philology, mathematics, fiction writing, and psychotherapy, respectively.

Still, I recall reading that Charles Darwin described the eminent scientists of his day as "mere schoolboys compared to old Aristotle!" I would discover the same thing when I encountered the writings of Thomas Aquinas in my early forties: that the atheists I had been reading were mere schoolboys (and a schoolgirl—Rand) compared to old Aquinas!

More than 700 years ago, Thomas had shot gaping holes in what I assumed were airtight atheist arguments, building upon the work of theologians and philosophers who had lived centuries before him. The Catholic answers, we might call them, to my atheism were always there waiting for me within the writings of the Church I grew up in—and I hadn't had a clue! Hence, part of my mission since then has been to disseminate Thomas's "golden wisdom" (as some popes have called it) far and wide.

Shortly after I came back to the Faith in 2004, I read Pope Leo XIII's 1879 encyclical *Aeterni Patris: Of the Restoration of Christian Philosophy According to the Mind of St. Thomas Aquinas, the Angelic Doctor* (since it was reproduced at the beginning of the first edition of the *Summa* I had acquired). The pope wrote in that encyclical that for whoever has rejected the Faith and claims to follow reason as his only guide, nothing will be more powerful in drawing him back, after God's supernatural grace, than the writings of the Church Fathers and Scholastics, most prominently those of Thomas Aquinas. Indeed, 125 years later, that was exactly the course I followed, as the Holy Spirit's stirrings and Thomas's writings drew me back to Christ and his Church after twenty-five years of atheism.

So a rational, *Thomistic* approach can be valuable in establishing common ground and drawing to Christ unbelievers who do not acknowledge the authority of Scripture, but who still honor reason and love truth. The powers of Thomas's reason can indeed persuade some people that faith is eminently reasonable, beautiful, and true, inspiring them to take the leap toward faith.

I will note as well that perhaps even more than Thomas's terse but famous *five ways* to prove the existence of God, which we'll discuss in chapter 2, it was Thomas's extensive analysis of God's attributes—the stuff of our chapters 3 through 26—that helped draw me back to the fullness of the truth of Christ and his Church. It was within Thomas's answers to those questions that I found that just as the mythical Paris, guided by the god Apollo, fatally pierced Achilles's heel with his arrow, Thomas, working in the city of Paris, guided by God almighty, pierced with arrows of truth the Achilles heel of the atheists' arguments, old and new, way back in the thirteenth century.

So, to the atheist who declares, "There is no God!", the perfect question to ask to get a conversation rolling is, indeed, "What is God?" In essence, "Just what (or who) do you propose does not exist?"

For the theist, who believes in God, and the Catholic, who also loves him as a Father, the same question is worth pondering. Consider the case of St. Rose of Lima, patroness of Peru. Since she was no formally trained philosopher or theologian, she once asked her priest confessor to compile for her a list of 150 perfections of God. (We'll touch on God's perfection soon, in chapter 4.) The list would become the focus of one of her favorite prayers, as she frequently spent hours in meditation on God's justice, mercy, omnipotence, wisdom, etc. Rose said this kind of prayer was pleasing to God and hateful to the devils that sometimes tormented her. She would be rewarded with many ecstatic visions during her brief life.

Perhaps Thomas's rigorous rational explanations in the pages ahead will open the path not only to a better understanding of the awesomeness of God, but also to a deeper prayer life in joyful union with him. (At least I hope and pray so!)

God awaits. Let's begin.

PART I

WHAT IS THE STUDY OF GOD?

It was necessary for man's salvation
that there should be a knowledge revealed
by God, besides philosophical science
built up by human reason.

ST, I, Q. 1., a. 1

THE SACRED SCIENCE OF
THEOLOGY

Sacred doctrine is a science.

ST, I, Q. 1., a. 2

St. Thomas commences his more than 1.5-million-word answer to the question "What is God?" (and the thousands of questions that flow from it) by addressing the issue of the proper study of questions about God—what we commonly call *theology*, from the Greek *theos* for God and *logos* for reason, and what Thomas calls in the Latin *sacra doctrina* (sacred doctrine). I will use the more familiar term in all but the first of our questions below.

Thomas says we need to investigate the nature and extent of sacred doctrine, which raises ten key questions. I'll condense his answers to keep them terse, but let's see now at least the gist of how Thomas unlocked all ten of them.

1 Is sacred doctrine necessary in addition to philosophy?

Some theologians in our day use the term *natural theology* to describe what we can know about God through the powers of unaided human reason (what Thomas called *philosophical science*), and they use the term *revealed theology* to describe what we can know about God through what God divinely revealed to us as written down in Scripture (Thomas's *sacred doctrine*). In any event, Thomas answered that sacred doctrine is necessary, in addition to philosophy. Philosophy, or unaided reason, can indeed discover some important truths about God, but it does so in a gradual and limited way. It would require so much time, diligence, and mental dexterity that its truths would be known only by a limited number of people. God's revelation teaches us truths that exceed human reason and is there to guide us to salvation.

If you'll permit an important digression, I should note that in this book, covering the first twenty-six questions of the *Summa*, which zero in on the existence, nature, and attributes of God, philosophy, or natural theology, will factor prominently. Thomas grounds his fundamental arguments on the power of reason alone (though he often references verses from Scripture to show how reason and revelation point to the same conclusions). Such issues and arguments are sometimes called *preambula fidei*, the preambles of faith, the highest truths we can reach about God through philosophy and natural (reason-based) theology.

So a Thomistic approach grounded in philosophy or natural theology can be valuable in establishing common ground and drawing sincerely truth-seeking unbelievers to Christ. On the other hand, those who already love God and cherish his written word will find these pages suffused with the holy wisdom of Sacred Scripture as well!

2 Is theology a science?

Yes. Although the articles of faith are not self-evident and some people deny them, some sciences (organized disciplines or bodies of knowledge) depend on principles known by a higher science. As musicians accept principles taught by mathematics—symmetry, counting, tempo, and so on—so theology is established upon principles revealed directly by God. Theologians apply reason based on these higher principles of revelation.

3 Is theology one science?

Theology is one, unified science or body of knowledge. Although it studies creatures—angels, corporal beings—and also human morality, it studies God primarily and created beings and all the rest only insofar as they relate to God. (Our focus in the pages of this book will be upon that primary study of God himself.)

4 Is theology a practical science?

Yes, in a real, but only a secondary sense. Theology is primarily a *speculative* (what we might call *abstract* or *theoretical*) science, rather than a practical science, because its primary aim is knowledge about God, rather than human acts. Still, it is both speculative and practical, in helping man toward his salvation, in which he will attain the perfect knowledge of God (the *beatific vision*), which will provide eternal bliss.

5 Is theology the highest and noblest of sciences?

Theology is indeed the highest and noblest of sciences. As we read in Scripture, "Wisdom . . . has sent out her maids to call from the highest places in the town" (Prov. 9:3). Other sciences are the handmaids of theology. Theology is higher and nobler than other sciences because it studies truths that are more certain, being based upon God's revelation, and because its subject matter is of the highest worth, its subject being God.

6 Is theology the same as wisdom?

Theology is wisdom above all human wisdom. Wisdom orders and judges things according to higher principles, as the architect who plans a house is wiser than the laborers who assemble the wood or the stones. God is the architect and highest cause of the whole universe, so the study of God is the highest of wisdom.

7 Is God the object of the science of theology?

As noted in our third question about theology being *one* science, in the sacred science of theology, all things in the universe are studied as they relate to God as their origin and their end. So, yes!

8 *Does theology use rational arguments?*

Theology rightly uses arguments. It does not argue to prove articles held by faith, but it does use the articles to prove other things, as St. Paul argues from the resurrection of Christ to demonstrate the truth of the general resurrection (1 Cor. 15). Arguments from human authority are the weakest; arguments from divine revelation are the strongest. So, yes, theology uses rational arguments.

9 *Should Holy Scripture use metaphor?*

Yes. Holy Scripture transcends the rational arguments based on human reason, and it rightly uses metaphors because comparisons of spiritual realities with material things help us to comprehend spiritual truths.

For a very simple example—from me, not from Thomas— when Mary says of God, "He has shown strength with his arm" (Luke 1:51), she means not that God has gigantic biceps, but that he, though spirit, is immensely powerful.

Further, some things taught metaphorically in some parts of Scripture, such as in types or prefigurements, are taught more directly in other parts. There are a vast number of these in Scripture. Consider, for one early and important example, how the mysterious priest Melchizedek's sacrifice of bread and wine (Gen. 14:18-20; Heb. 6:20, 7:17) prefigures Jesus' explanation and institution of the sacrament of the Eucharist (Matt. 26:26-29; Mark 14:22-25; Luke 22:19-20; John 6; 1 Cor. 11:23-26).

10 Does Holy Scripture have multiple levels of meaning?

Indeed! For example, the same sentence can describe a fact and reveal a mystery.

Interpreting Scripture should start at the *historical* or *literal* sense. Based upon the literal level is the *spiritual* sense, whereby particular things, people, or events described by the words of the text also point to other spiritual realities. (For example, Thomas tells elsewhere that when Jesus told his disciples to ask God for their "daily bread" in Matthew 6:11, that bread also signifies the bread that would become the "bread of life" after Jesus would initiate the sacrament of the holy Eucharist.) Within the spiritual sense, things of the Old Law that signify or point to things of the New Law constitute the *allegorical* sense. Things that signify what we ought to do and how we are to live constitute the *moral* sense. Things that relate to or point to the glory of eternal life constitute the *anagogical* sense.

Summa of Sacred Science

Theology (sacred science) . . .

1 is necessary in addition to philosophy based on human reason alone.

2 is a science (an organized body of knowledge).

3 is one, unified science with its primary focus on God.

4 is primarily a speculative science aimed at knowledge of God, but is a practical science in a secondary sense in that

it has the most important implications for how we live our lives on the road to salvation.

5 is the noblest of all the sciences since it studies the most certain truths about the loftiest subject matter.

6 is above human wisdom as it pursues divine wisdom.

7 has God as its object, whereas all things in the universe are studied as they relate to him as their origin and end.

8 rightly uses rational arguments.

9 rightly studies the use of metaphor in Scripture.

10 rightly studies both the multiple levels of meaning in Scripture, in the historical or literal sense as well as in the spiritual sense, which includes the allegorical, moral, and anagogical sense.

This ends our preparatory consideration of the nature of theology, both in its philosophical domain of natural theology and in the divine realm of revealed theology, the *sacra doctrina* based on what God has shown and told us.

Before we begin our full-blown consideration of just "what is God?", Thomas would first have us consider "is God?", in my words, and in his words, "Whether God Exists?" (*ST*, I, Q. 2, Prologue). Just how can we know that there does exist a God whom we can study? Let's find out in Part II.

IS THERE A GOD TO STUDY?

It is said in the person of God,
"I am who am."

ST, I, Q. 2, a. 3

2

HOW WE CAN KNOW GOD
EXISTS

The existence of God can be proved in five ways.

ST, I, Q. 2., a. 3

1 *Is God's existence self-evident?*

St. Thomas tells us (*ST*, I, Q. 2., a. 1) that people argue that the existence of God is self-evident and undeniable because of one or more of the following:

> **A** knowledge of God is implanted in us by nature (as St. John Damascene noted);

B as soon as the statement "God exists" is understood, his existence cannot be denied, because the word *God* means that thing than which nothing greater can be thought, but what exists in reality is greater than that which exists only mentally (as St. Anselm argued); or

C the existence of truth is self-evident and cannot be denied.

But, as Thomas notes, none of these contentions holds water.

Regarding the first point, an awareness of God *is* implanted in our nature, but in a confused way. It is one thing to know that someone approaches and another thing to know that it is (for example) Peter. All people seek happiness, but not all realize that our complete happiness (*beatitude*) lies only in God. Further, *to mentally grasp the idea* of a being than whom nothing greater can be imagined does not prove that such a being *actually exists*. In fact, we know there are people who will not admit that God exists.

Regarding the third point, which is a little thorny, Thomas notes that per Aristotle, we cannot mentally admit the opposite of what is self-evident—for example, that a part is greater than the whole—but people do deny that God exists. As Scripture tells us, "The fool said in his heart, there is no God" (Ps. 52:1).* God's existence *would be* self-evident

---

* Please note that Thomas used a biblical translation based on the Latin Vulgate, and the fathers of the English Dominican Province translated the *Summa Theologica* into English in 1911. Some of the wording of texts, names of Bible books (e.g., Ecclesiasticus or Ecclus. for Sirach and Apocalypse or Apoc. for Revelation), and numbering of verses differ from some modern English translations. For those who would like to track down the verses cited in the *Summa*, the English translation most similar to the Bible Thomas used is the Douay-Rheims edition, which translates the Latin Vulgate.

to us *if* God's essence were understood (since, as we will see in the next chapter, his existence and essence are one), but God's essence is imperfectly known to man, and our imperfect knowledge is achieved through reasoned argument and through revelation.

Finally, that truth in general exists is self-evident; this cannot be rationally denied. Yet the existence of one primal truth who is God is *not* self-evident to us.

2 *Can God's existence by proven through reason?*

Although Thomas argues that God's existence is *not self-evident* to us, in his next article, he argues that his existence *can indeed be proved through reason* alone. St. Paul tells us of God that "ever since the creation of the world his invisible nature, namely, his eternal power and deity, has been clearly perceived in the things that have been made" (Rom. 1:20). The Catholic Church agrees. The First Vatican Council would declare as dogma that certain knowledge of God can be attained "through the light of reason," and we read in our current *Catechism of the Catholic Church* that "by natural reason man can know God with certainty, on the basis of his works" (50).

Thomas declares, "The existence of God can be proved in five ways." (I like to think they are "as easy as 1-2-3"— not that they are so easy, but because we can find them in *ST,* I, Q. 2, a. 3!) Here Thomas tersely presents, in just a couple of pages, five proofs that he explicates in more detail in other writings, most notably his *Summa Contra Gentiles.*

Thomas begins with a couple of objections. One states that God's existence cannot be proved by reason because God is supposedly infinitely good, yet there is evil in the world (the age-old *problem of evil*). Another holds that "it is superfluous to suppose that what can be accounted for by a few principles has been produced by many." (That's a concept prescient of *Occam's razor*, a principle elucidated by William of Occam, a Franciscan born about thirteen years after Thomas's death.) In brief, all of our reason relies on natural phenomena—what we can sense—but we can explain natural phenomena by nature itself, and therefore, we don't need to bring in God.

Thomas argues to the contrary that we can indeed prove God's existence through reason, and then he briefly lists five ways. Before I describe them in our next question, let's note two important characteristics about all of them.

First, they all employ *a posteriori* reasoning. That is, they start with the undeniable *evidence of our human senses* and then *rigorously reason backward* from these phenomena to their *ultimate cause*. In other words, they do *not* begin upon some abstract philosophical premise with which we may or may not agree.

Second, many pagan philosophers believed that the universe itself was not created, but existed always, whether or not with God. Thomas believes that *reason alone* could not address whether the universe was created, though we know definitively through revelation that it was. Nonetheless, all five of his arguments are designed to prove God's existence *even if* the universe existed eternally with God. Even if the universe were not created in time, the universe could not be *sustained* in existence without the causal power of God! Further, there is no possibility that God created the world and then left it alone as he went about other business. All movement or change, causation, perfection, order, and purpose require a Prime Mover, first efficient cause, necessary being, ultimate formal cause, and final cause for their existence—not merely sometime in the past, but *at this very moment.*

"We live, and move, and have our being" (Acts. 17:28) right now through the grace, love, and power of an eternal God. Now let's look at the five proofs.

3 *What are Thomas's five ways to prove the existence of God?*

Please be aware that I present them here summarized in the most concise of nutshells. To examine them more deeply, please see *ST,* I, Q. 2, a. 3 and consult some of the writings of the greatest modern philosophical minds who have explained them in depth (Fr. Reginald Garrigou-Lagrange, Etienne Gilson, and Edward Feser being among my favorites).

Note as well that to fully grasp them requires a deep understanding of fundamental Aristotelean-Thomistic principles, including the distinction between *potency* and *act* (potentiality and actuality) and the nature of *the four causes* (material, formal, efficient, and final)—a comprehension I have never encountered in the writings of modern atheists who try to discredit the proofs. Now let's get ready to find God in five ways through the powers of reason he so graciously gave us.

> A **The argument from motion or change**: Our senses tell us with certainty that some things are in motion. They change, such as in their location or in qualities such as size and temperature. They move from some state of *potentiality* (what they could change into) to an *actuality* (what they actually are).

Anything that moves from a potentiality to an actuality must be made actual by something else. A thing cannot *give* what it does not already *have*. These outside sources of change cannot go on indefinitely, though, so there must be a first agent of change, a *first mover* to put the series of changes in motion, as a stick moves something else only because it is put in motion by a hand. There must be a first, unmoved mover, *already completely actualized* and put in motion by no other. This mover we call God.

B **The argument from efficient cause:** Our senses reveal an order of efficient causes in the natural world by examining the effects produced. A thing cannot cause itself, because then it would exist prior to itself, which is impossible. The chain of causation cannot go into infinity because without a first cause, no intermediate causes would exist, and to take away the cause is to take away the effect. But there clearly are effects. Therefore, there must be a first efficient, uncaused cause, and this we call God.

C **The argument from necessary being:** We find in nature things that are possible to be or not to be—things that come to be, but pass away. (Who among us gave himself his own existence or will live on earth eternally?) If everything in the universe is possible not to be (that is, is *contingent*, being dependent on something else), at one time there could have been no existing thing. If that were true, there would be nothing now, because something that does not exist cannot give itself its own existence. There must therefore be some being that not merely *possibly*, but *necessarily* exists, having received its existence not from another thing, but which causes other things to exist. We call this necessary being God.

D **The argument from degrees of being:** Everything that exists has some measure of goodness by the fact that it exists. (It is truly better to be than not to be!) Still, we clearly see that some things in the world are better than others. They are more good, noble, true, or complete. (Consider, for example, the increasing powers and abilities of living organisms as we move from plants to animals to human beings.) But there is no standard to appreciate degrees of perfection unless there is an unchanging maximum. There must be some utmost being against whom we measure the various goodness and perfections in every other being. This standard of perfection we call God.

E **The argument from the governance of the world** (also known as the argument from *final cause*): There are an order and seemingly purposeful behavior even in inanimate natural bodies that follow the regular laws of nature. Although they lack awareness, they act in the same way, over and over again, in ways that achieve effective ends or goals. Unintelligent beings cannot reach specific goals unless directed by a being with intelligence, "as the arrow is shot to its mark by the archer. Therefore, some intelligent being exists by whom all natural things are directed to their end; and this being we call God."

In essence, Thomas's five ways prove not that God well may exist, but that *he absolutely must exist*. Otherwise, the world brought to us by our senses, our own selves and senses included, simply could not exist.

For those who recall that Thomas started his article with objections against God's existence based on the existence of evil and the idea that nature needs no explanation, Thomas responds to the first with the argument from St. Augustine that since God is indeed the highest good, he would only permit evil to exist in his works if his omnipotence and goodness were such that he could bring goodness even out of evil. Thomas notes, "This is part of the infinite goodness of God, that he should allow evil to exist, and out of it produce good."

As for nature explaining its own existence, Thomas responds that nature works for particular goals or ends only as determined by a higher *agent* (a being with the capacity to act), so whatever nature does can be traced back to God, *the first cause*. Indeed, even the voluntary acts of human beings can be traced back to a higher cause than human reason and will "since these can change and fail; for all things that are changeable and capable of defect must be traced back to an *immovable and self-necessary first principle*, as was shown in the body of the article."

WHAT IS
GOD?

When the existence of a thing
has been ascertained, there remains the
further question of the manner of its existence,
in order that we may know its essence.

ST, I, Q. 3, Prologue

PROLOGUE

Because we cannot know what God is,
but rather what he is not, we have no means for
considering how God is, but rather how he is not.

ST, I, Q. 3, Prologue

St. Thomas usually starts each of his *questions* (the equivalent of this book's *chapters*) with a brief *prologue* that sets the stage for the issues he will address. Since his Question 3, "On the Simplicity of God," begins to directly answer his (and our) fundamental question of "What is God?", a brief prologue to our Part III seems in order.

Now we consider the difference between knowing *that* God is and knowing *what* God is—or is not—and what a difference that makes! Having established the five ways, based on the evidence of effects in the world, that a being we call God *must exist*, we are now poised to directly face that question Thomas so famously posed as a child.

How startling it is, as we saw in our second opening quotation, that a mature Thomas would write, "Because we cannot know what God is, but rather what he is not, we have no means for considering how God is, but rather how he is not." But there is no need for worry or for disappointment. This book need not end after only a couple dozen pages!

This important and productive method for thinking about God is called the *via negativa* ("negative way") of theology, or, if you want to get fancy, the *apophatic* method, from the Greek *apo* for "other than" and *phanai* for "speak"—that is, to argue by means of denial.

Thomas starts his examination of God with the method of negative theology to help us know some important things about what God is *not* by considering some attributes that could not possibly describe a Prime Mover, a necessary being who is pure act. In proving, for example, that God is in no way complex or composed of any parts, we achieve some sense of God's utter *simplicity* (the stuff of our next chapter). In proving he cannot change, we see that he must be *immutable* (chapter 9).

The insights we attain are never complete, though—not here on earth, and not even on heaven, when we shall see God face to face in the beatific vision. Even then, God's utter vastness exceeds beyond measure the comprehension of even the glorified human intellect (though it will still bring us total bliss). Still, Thomas's insights are so powerful that they can move some unbelievers to God (as they did for me).

3

GOD IS
SIMPLE

The absolute simplicity of God
may be shown in many ways.

ST, I, Q. 3, a. 7

How intriguing that whereas some modern atheists attack
the idea of God because he would have to be unimagin-
ably *complex*,* Thomas, using the negative way, concludes
that God's first fundamental attribute is his utter *simplicity*.
This simplicity can be seen in many ways . . . that are not

---

* See, for example, Richard Dawkins's *The God Delusion*, 176–180.

necessarily so simple to explain in brief! Nonetheless, with Thomas's help, let us begin to count the ways.

1 Does God have a body?

Some have argued from Scripture that God does indeed have a body. Job 11:8-9 tells us about God's *dimensions*, in that he is higher than heaven, deeper than Sheol, longer than the earth, and broader than the sea. Gen. 1:26 declares that man is made in God's *image and likeness*, and we all know that *we have bodies*. And what about God's *body parts*, like his arm (Job. 40:9), his eyes and face (Ps. 34 [33]:15-16), and his right hand (Ps. 118 [117]:16)? Further, you can't assume *postures* without a body, but God sits on his throne (Isa. 6:1) and stands up to judge (3:13).

Thomas answers that God is *not* composed of body and spirit. He has no body.* Scripture tells us "God is a spirit" (John 4:24), and reason tells us, "No body is in motion unless it be put in motion." But God is the first and unmoved mover, so nothing can have put him in motion.

And let us not forget how we saw that Scripture uses metaphor (Q. 1, a. 9). Scriptural references to God's size or to body parts like his arm or hand are metaphorical references to his vastness, power, etc. Likewise regarding his postures. "He is spoken of as sitting, on account of his unchangeableness and dominion; and as standing, on account of his power of overcoming whatever withstands him."

---

* That revelation shows that God the Son assumed a human body for our salvation is a separate issue. In a similar manner, Thomas writes elsewhere in the *Summa* in his Treatise on the Angels (ST, I, Qs. 50-64), that angels are also spiritual beings without bodies, yet they can assume human bodily form when carrying out special missions for God.

As for being made in God's image and likeness, God holds dominion over all of creation. We are told in Genesis 1:26 that God gave us dominion over all other creatures on earth. This is on account of our *intelligence* and powers of *reasoning*. These are *incorporeal* (spiritual, not bodily), and through these powers we are made in God's image and likeness.

2 *Is God composed of matter and form?*

For a quick Aristotelian/Thomistic (and Catholic) primer on matter and form, *matter* is that *out of which* a thing is made, and *form* is that *into which* the thing is made. In human beings, our *bodies* are made of *matter*, and our *souls* are the form that gives us life and determines what we are and what powers we possess as human beings. Indeed, per the *Catechism*,

> the unity of the soul and body is so profound that one has to consider the soul to be the "form" of the body—i.e., it is because of its spiritual soul that the body made of matter becomes a living, human body; spirit and matter, in man, are not two natures, united, but rather their union forms a single nature (364).

Unlike us, however, God is *not* a composite of matter and form, because matter is a *potential* made actual by form, and God has no potential, being *pure act*. "Whatever is primarily and essentially an agent must be primarily and essentially form. Now God is the first agent, since he is the first *efficient* cause. He is therefore of his essence a form, and not composed of matter and form."

To expand on the previous discussion of matter and form,

in the Aristotelian/Thomistic explanation of the *four causes*, the *material cause* is that "*out of* which" something is made, the *formal cause* is "that *into* which something is made," the *efficient cause* is "that *by* which something is made," and the *final cause* is that "for the *sake* of which" something is made.

For a simple example, pieces of wood (material cause) are cut and assembled into a flat top and four legs (formal cause) by the efforts of a carpenter (efficient cause), so someone can have a table to sit at and place his food on for eating (final cause). The carpenter, the efficient cause, is also called the active agent, derived from the Latin *agere* for "doing," for he is the one whose actions give the wood its form as a table.

The wood itself, composed of matter, is *potentially* a vast number of things besides a table. God, being completely form, has no *potential* to become something else, since he alone is already and always fully actualized, pure act, first agent, and first efficient cause (as we saw in Thomas's second proof from effects—and as we saw in the fifth proof, the ultimate final cause as well).

3   Is God the same as his nature or essence?

This one can be a bit of a brain-twister. Indeed, I wonder how many of us would have thought to even ask it (or the next one)!

Thomas begins by citing Scripture: "I am the way, the truth, and the life" (John 14:6). He says that God declares he is *life itself*, and *not* only *a living thing*. "Now the relation between Godhead and God is the same as the relation between life and a living thing. Therefore, God is his very Godhead."

If I might elaborate, you, dear reader, are a man or a

woman, but not humanity itself. You *have* a human *nature*, but you are *not* human nature itself, because you have your own particular matter that is your unique body—what Thomas calls the *suppositum proprium*.* Recall that God, as we saw two questions back, has no body. God is identical to his nature or essence in a way that no creature can be. As Thomas tells us, "God is his very Godhead."

4   Is God's essence or nature different from his existence?

God does *not* have a separate essence and existence, although it is one thing *for us* to know *that* God *exists*, and quite another to know *what* he is (his *essence*). The two are quite the same in him.

Thomas begins his response to objections by quoting St. Hilary of Poitiers (c. 310–367): "In God existence is not an accidental quality, but subsisting truth." Therefore, what subsists in God is his existence.

Thomas notes that whatever anything has besides its essence must be caused either *from within* by the constituent principles that make up its essence (for example, in humans, the capacity to laugh is caused by the constituent principles of human nature), or *from without* by some exterior agent, "as heat is caused in water by fire."

Now, no thing's existence could be caused by its interior constituent principles, since no thing can be the sufficient

---

* "The proper or particular individual substance," per Roy J. Deferrari, *A Latin-English Dictionary of St. Thomas Aquinas: Based on the Summa Theologica and Selected Passages of His Other Works* (Boston: St. Paul Editions, 1986), p. 1,019.

cause of its own existence. (As a Scholastic philosophical saying goes, "You can't give what you don't have.") Therefore, any thing whose existence is different from its essence must be brought into existence from without, by something else. This cannot apply to God because, as we saw in the second proof, he is the "first efficient cause. Therefore, it is impossible that in God his existence should differ from his essence."

Further, existence is what makes potential things actual or real. Essences like humanity are called actual because they exist. *Existence is to essence as actuality is to potentiality.* "Therefore, since in God there is no potentiality . . . it follows that his essence does not differ from existence. Therefore, his essence is his existence." Let us recall as well from our third proof that God is *necessary being.* His nature is not only that he can exist, but that he must!

5 *Can God be placed in a genus?*

For some, this may suggest a further question: "What's a genus?" "Good question," I say.

Let's consider the case, not of God, but of *man*, and then of *gods*, as we define *genus* and *species*. Biological creatures are typically classified into genus and species in various ways. Aristotle and other philosophers defined humans as *rational animals*, for example. In this case, the genus or "class" is that of animals, sensate living creatures who can move about, and the species identifier is "rational," the fact that humans alone possess the power of rational thought (a fundamental way in which we were made in the image and likeness of God). In a similar vein, modern biologists call us *Homo sapiens*, the genus *homo* referring to two-legged hominid (primate) creatures and *sapiens*, from the Latin *sapientia*, defining us as "wise." We are then the "wise primates" (or at least potentially so!).

We could do the same, at least grammatically, for members of the mythological pantheon of gods, like Zeus and Odin, perhaps, by defining either as the "chief or ruling god" of their polytheistic system. Thomas tells us, however, that the God we are led to by reason, and by revelation as well, is so fundamentally different from any mythological god that he alone is no member of any broader class of similar beings. God is utterly unique. No wonder he commanded us, "You shall have no other gods before me" (Exod. 20:2; Deut. 5:7).

Thomas tells us that God cannot be classed as a particular kind or member of any group or category. Members of a class share an essence but differ in some manner of their existence—but remember: we just saw that God's essence and existence are one.

6 Is there anything accidental in God?

I know that you are a rational human being made in the image and likeness of God, but I do not know if your eyes are blue or brown. Your intellectual soul is the *essence* of your humanity, whereas your eye color is an *accident*. This does not mean your eyes are their color without good reason—reasons Catholic priest Gregor Mendel, the "Father of Genetics," helped us all see clearly. Thomas says, "A subject is compared to its accidents as potentiality to actuality; for a subject is in some sense made actual by its accidents."

We are now awaiting the arrival of a new grandson. Our

son has one gene for blue eyes from me and one for brown eyes from his mother (who we believe has two genes for brown eyes). Since the gene for brown eyes is "dominant," his eyes are brown. Our daughter-in-law has blue eye genes from both parents. Our new grandbaby's eye color remains a mystery to us right now, to be determined by the roll of the genetic dice. Yet when those dice stopped rolling at conception, that particular pairing of genes made the *potential* eye color (blue or brown) *actual*.*

Now, keeping in mind that eye color is merely one of a myriad of "accidents" that differentiate us as individual human beings, Thomas tells us that God does not have any *accidents* at all—nothing that actualizes any kind of *potential*—because *God is always fully actualized*! His essence is his own existence, to which nothing can be added. Further, consider that "accidents are caused by the constituent principles of the subject." (In our example, human eye color is caused by genes.) Lest we forget, "there can be nothing caused in God, since he is the first cause. Hence it follows that there is no accident in God."

7 Does God have parts?

Some argued that God is complex and made of many parts, because whatever God made imitates him in its goodness, and no living being is altogether simple, without any parts. Further, it appears that composites are better than simple things, as chemical compounds are better than their simple elements and animals are better than any of the body parts

---

* They came out blue. (And a few months later, a brown-eyed girl joined our family, courtesy of her two brown-eyed parents.)

that compose them. Therefore, they reasoned, God must have parts and cannot be completely simple.

Thomas answers, however, that we can show God's *absolute simplicity* in many ways. Let's take a quick look at the first four.

A As we saw in all the previous articles, God has no body. He is not composed of matter and form. His nature does not differ from his essence, nor his essence from his existence. He is not composed of genus and species, nor of subject and accident. "Therefore, it is clear that God is nowise composite, but is altogether simple."

B Every composite comes *after* its component parts and depends on them, but God is the *first* being.

C Every composite is *caused*, because different things cannot unite unless something causes them to come together, but, as we've seen, God is *uncaused*, since he is the first efficient cause.

D Every composite consists of *potentiality and actuality*, but God is *fully actual*.

As for the opening objections, though every created thing imitates God in some limited way, it does so according to its own essence, which, unlike God's, is composite and differs from its existence. As for composites being better than simple things, it works that way for created things because they all contain partial aspects of goodness that cannot be found in any single thing. "But the perfection of the divine goodness is found in one simple thing." If I might explicate this idea with a profound passage found later in the *Summa* (I, Q. 47, a. 1), Thomas writes:

> He produced many and diverse creatures, that what was wanting to one in the representation of the divine goodness might be supplied by another. For goodness, which in God is simple and uniform, in creatures is manifold and divided and hence the whole universe together participates in the divine goodness more perfectly, and represents it better than any single creature.

8 *Does God become part of other things?*

Another important aspect of his simplicity is that *God does not enter into the composition of other things.* Not only does God have no parts, but he is certainly not part of anything else. Some said in the time of St. Augustine (that is, the fifth century), as Thomas cites and some New Age disciples say even now, that God is the "world-soul" or the "soul of the highest heaven."

But God exists not *in* or *as* the universe, but as its creator and sustainer. Indeed, this subject seems to have raised the ire of the normally placid Angelic Doctor. Here Thomas lists by name one David of Dinant, "who most absurdly taught that God was primary matter." David's pantheistic doctrine taught that matter, intellect, and God are all actually one and the same. Thomas says David could not have been more wrong: "For matter is merely potential and potentiality is absolutely posterior to actuality." God, as we've seen again and again, is pure actuality. (God only knows what was the matter with David of Dinant's intellect!)

A Simple Summa of God's Simplicity

(Or how the negative way can give us something positive to say!)

(*ST*, I, 3, aa. 1–8)

God . . .	Therefore, God . . .
has no body	is spiritual
is not composed of mater and form	is pure form
does not have a separate essence or nature	is the same as his essence or nature
does not have a separate essence and existence	is his own essence and existence
is not a member of a class or genus	is utterly unique and beyond genus
does not have accidental, potential characteristics	is completely actualized substance
has no parts	is absolutely simple
is not a part of anything else	is absolutely primal being

4

GOD IS
PERFECT

All created perfections are in God.
Hence he is spoken of as universally perfect.

ST, I, Q. 4, a. 2

St. Thomas says that after considering God's simplicity, he
will move next to God's perfection, and since every perfect
thing is called good, first, he will examine the "divine perfection," and then (in our next chapter) the "divine goodness."

1 Is God perfect?

Some argued that God should not be said to be perfect because *perfection* is an attribute applied to something that is completely made (the Latin *perfectus*, deriving from *per* for "completely" and *facere* for "to do or make"), and God was not made. Another argument against God's perfection held that God is the first source of all things, but beginnings seem imperfect, as a seed is imperfect compared to the plant that grows from it.

Thomas commences his logical arguments with a direct appeal to Scripture: "You, therefore, must be perfect, as your heavenly Father is perfect" (Matt. 5:48).

He then cites some ancient philosophers who held that the "first principle" was *not* best and most perfect, but this was because they considered only *material* principles. *Matter*, as we have seen, is merely potential and indeed most imperfect. It requires *form* to become some particular existing thing. God, as we saw in Q. 3, a. 2, has no matter and is pure form. "Hence, the first acting principle needs to be most actual, and therefore most perfect; for a thing is perfect in proportion to its state of actuality, because we call that perfect which lacks nothing of its mode of perfection." As we saw in Q. 3., a. 6, God is completely actualized and has no potentiality.

Thomas cites an interesting passage from Pope St. Gregory the Great, when addressing the first objection about *perfection* meaning "completely made": "Though our lips can only stammer, we yet chant the high things of God." In other words, our normal language falls short when speaking of God. Still, Thomas notes that created things are called *perfect* when they move from their potential to their fullest actuality. So, in the sense that perfection denotes anything that lacks nothing in its actuality, the word does indeed apply to God.

Now, as for God being the source or beginning of all things and hence seemingly imperfect, no *material* principle is perfect or "absolutely primal." Even the seed, though it is the principle of life, has come from a plant or animal previous to it, since a potential being can be "reduced to act" (made actual) only by something that is actual. God is that fully actualized (that is, perfect) first principle who is the beginning (and end—final cause) of all things.

As modern Thomist Brian Davies, O.P. sums it up: "God is not something capable of improvement."[4] God could not possibly be better than he is.

2 Are the perfections of all things present within God?

The most fundamental argument that the perfections of all things could not exist within God holds that the perfections of created things are *many* and *diverse* (think of the brilliance of the sun, the towering majesty of a mountain, or the tender innocence of a newborn baby), yet we have seen that God is completely *simple* (Q. 3).

Thomas argues to the contrary, beginning with a quotation from Dionysius*: "God in his one existence prepossess all things."

---

* Author of works including *On the Divine Names* (which Thomas cites here) and *The Celestial Hierarchy*. Believed in the Middle Ages to be St. Dionysius the Areopagite, converted by St. Paul (Acts 17:34). He is usually referred to now as Pseudo-Dionysius or Pseudo-Denys and is believed to be a late fifth- to early sixth-century Christian theologian and philosopher who wrote under the name St. Dionysius. *Areopagite* refers a rock called the Areopagus (Ares's rock), near the acropolis in Athens, where Paul preached.

Thomas tells us that all created perfections exist first within God. God is called *universally perfect* and lacks nothing. He explains that whatever perfection is found in an effect must be found in its *effective cause*. We see this in agents (effective causes) that are *univocal* (of the same kind as their effects), as when a human produces a human, or, "in a more eminent degree," in agents that are "equivocal" (of a different kind from their effects), as when the sun's power produces various effects upon the variety of living species on earth, from enabling plants to grow through photosynthesis to keeping our bodies from freezing and helping us get a nice tan! Effects "pre-exist virtually" their efficient causes.

It is true that effects pre-existing virtually in a *material cause* do so in an *imperfect* way, since matter is imperfect, whereas agency (efficient causation) is perfect. Still, to pre-exist virtually in an *efficient cause* is to exist in a *perfect* way. So, since God is the first efficient cause of all things, "the perfections of all things must pre-exist in God in a more imminent way." Here, Thomas taps Dionysius's insights once more: "It is not that he is this and not that, but that he is all, as the cause of all."

In sum, there is no perfection in any creature that God, as the Creator of all good things, does not exceed. Indeed, every good in every created thing reflects in some small way the ultimate goodness of God. Because "God is the first effective cause of things, the perfections of all things must pre-exist in God in a more eminent way."

3 Can any creature be like God?

It may seem that no creature could be like God, considering scriptural passages like these: "There is none like thee among the gods, O Lord" (Ps. 86 [85]:8) and "To whom then will you liken God?" (Isa. 40:18). However, it is also written: "Let us make man in our image, after our likeness" (Gen. 1:26) and "When he appears we will be like him" (1 John 3:2).

Thomas states that likeness is based on an agreement or communication in form, and he drills down on three ways in which such likeness can vary.

A   Things are *equal* in likeness when they agree "according to the same formality, and according to the same mode," as when two things equally white are said to be alike in their whiteness. This is the most perfect or complete form of likeness.

B   Things may be *imperfect* in likeness when they agree in their form, but "not according to the same measure." For example, our two dogs Lucy (a miniature Schnauzer) and Lily (a miniature American Eskimo) shared this kind of likeness in that both were white in color. Lily, however, a veritable furry snowball, was whiter (white in a greater measure) than Lucy.

C   Things may also share a *generic* (but not specific) likeness when an agent and its effect are not of the same species. We saw this in the question above contrasting the way humans cause other humans (in their specific likeness) with how the sun is a causal agent for many forms of life (in the sun's generic likeness). Now, God transcends classification even within any *genus* (from which the term *generic* rises). Therefore, for an agent that transcends any genus, its effects will still more distantly reproduce the form of the agent, not, that is, so as to participate in the likeness of the agent's form according to the same specific or generic formality; but only according to some sort of analogy; as existence is common to all. In this way all created things, so far as they are beings, are like God as the first and universal principle of being.

Creatures, then, are like God not according to any commonality in genus or species, but only according to *analogy*, in that God is *essential being*, whereas creatures are *beings by participation in God's being*. Scripture recognizes that man is like God in this analogous way, but not in perfect likeness. Finally, although we can admit that creatures are in some ways like God, "it must nowise be admitted that God is like creatures." Dionysius has noted that "a mutual likeness can be found of things of the same order, but not between a cause and that which is caused."

As Thomas sums it up, "We say that a statue is like a man, but not conversely; so also a creature can be spoken of as in some sort like God; but not that God is like a creature."*

Summa of God's Perfection

God is . . .

1 fully actualized, is completely perfect, and could not possibly be better than he is.

2 the source of the lesser perfections that exist in any and all created beings.

3 the first and universal principle of being. Creatures are like him in limited ways, but he is unlike any creature.

---

* Perhaps we may find violations of this principle in modern philosophical theories that treat the body like a machine or the brain like a computer, rather than the other way around.

5

WHAT GOOD IS

*Goodness and being are really the same,
and differ only in idea.*

ST, I, Q. 5, a. 1

Did you ever hear or pray the semi-rhyming childhood prayer that begins "God is great. God is good. Let us thank him for this food"? Just what does it mean to say, "God is good?" St. Thomas agreed that God indeed is good, as we will see in our next chapter. But before presenting his case, Thomas thinks it best to first define our terms and examine just what we mean by the term *good*. He presents six articles in his Question 5, "Of Goodness in General."

To set the stage for our examination of the goodness of God, we'll follow Thomas's lead, but to avoid any lengthy detours, after our first question, I'll cut to the chase and summarize the remaining articles (hopefully doing a "good" enough job).

1 Is goodness really different from being?

It might seem at first that it is. Boethius wrote, "I perceive that in nature the fact that things are good is one thing: that they are is another." Further, nothing can be its own form, but according to the Arabic *Book of Causes* (once attributed to Aristotle), "That is called good which has the form of being." Finally, goodness can vary from more to less, but being cannot be more or less. Therefore, it appears that goodness truly differs from being.

Thomas pulls out the big guns on this one! First, he cites St. Augustine, who wrote that "inasmuch as we exist we are good." Thomas then states that goodness and being do differ *in idea* but "are really the same." He expounds that the "essence of goodness consists in that it is some way desirable." (The good is that which is wanted.) Next, he draws on the real Aristotle, who wrote in his *Nicomachean Ethics*, book 1, that "goodness is what all desire."

Thomas then connects goodness and perfection: "Now it is clear that a thing is desirable only insofar as it is perfect: for all desire their own perfection. But everything perfect is perfect as far as it is actual." Therefore, anything is perfect "so far as it exists; for it is existence that makes all things actual. . . Hence it is clear that goodness and being are the same really. But goodness presents the aspect of desirableness, which being does not present." In other words, they differ *in idea*, but not *really*.

To elaborate just a bit, every human being, at the primal level of being a person, has both being and goodness. As Augustine posited, everything that exists is good. The person who has developed his knowledge or virtue has actualized potential goodness and thereby grown in goodness, yet we can also say he has moved toward *being* all he can be.

2 *Does goodness come before being in our ideas?*

No. Thomas notes that Aristotle wrote rightly that "the first of created things is being."* Thomas elaborates that being is prior to goodness "in idea" (in the way we think). The meaning that is signified when we name a thing "is that which the mind conceives of the thing and intends by the word that stands for it."† What is prior in idea is what is first conceived by the intellect. Since everything we know is knowable only through the fact that it exists, the first thing conceived by intellect is being. Therefore, being is the proper object of the intellect, and is "primarily intelligible: as sound is the primary audible." Hence, being is prior to goodness in idea. And we need to know that something *exists* before we desire it for its *goodness*.

---

* This is another reference to the *Book of Causes*, upon which Thomas wrote a complete commentary, but which modern scholars no longer attribute to Aristotle.

† Indeed, within the Treatise on Man, in ST, I, Qs. 75-94, and especially Qs. 78 and 79 on the specific and intellectual powers of the soul, Thomas lays out a detailed analysis of human idea—or concept—formation. It is based on the *correspondence theory of truth*, whereby we arrive at truth when external reality and our conception of it match. Starting with the power of our senses and rising to the conceptual and rational powers of the intellect, Thomas posits, contrary to some modern philosophers, that ideas are not "that which we think about," but are "that by which we think about things." Properly formed ideas do not draw us away from, but connect us to reality.

3 Is every being good?

Thomas argues that every being that is not God is God's creature, and Scripture tells us clearly enough that "everything created by God is good" (1 Tim. 4:4). God is the greatest good, and we saw in our last question that every being participates in God's likeness. Thomas elaborates that every being is good by its being, since all being is *actuality* and is therefore in some way *perfect*. Perfection implies desirability and goodness, so "every being as such is good."

This question and its answer become especially interesting when Thomas addresses the second of four objections. The objection cites Isaiah 5:20: "Woe to those who call evil good and good evil," and concludes that some things are called evil, and therefore not every being is good. Thomas responds to this objection with a terse description of the nature of evil:

> No being can be spoken of as evil, formally as being, but only so far as it lacks being. Thus a man is said to be evil, because he lacks some virtue; and an eye is said to be evil, because it lacks the power to see well. Evil, then, does not possess an existence of its own, but denotes an *absence* of being that deprives a being of its perfect actualization.*

4 Does goodness act as a final cause?

Absolutely! Aristotle makes clear that the end or goal of a thing is "that for the sake of which something is." Thomas

---

* Indeed, Thomas will write in his Treatise on the Angels (*ST*, I, Q. 63, a. 4) that even Satan and the demons of hell are good in their nature by the fact that they exist but are evil through their own will in choosing not to love God. We will see how he addresses the issue in this book's chapter 8.

concludes that "since goodness is that which all things desire, and since this has the aspect of an end, it is clear that goodness implies the aspect of an end."

To adapt a modern idiom just a bit, goodness, we can rightly say, is "what makes the world go round."

5 Does goodness consist of mode, species, and order?

This perhaps strange-sounding question arises from Scripture: "But thou has arranged all things by measure and number and weight" (Wis. 11:20), and from a comment on it from Augustine: "Measure fixes the mode of everything, number gives it its species, and weight gives it rest and stability."

To make a long exegesis short, the Angelic Doctor (Thomas) agrees with the Doctor of Grace (Augustine) that "the essence of goodness consists in mode, species, and number." Thomas says, "A thing is said to be perfect according to the mode of its perfection."

Everything is what it is through its form (recall that a formal cause refers to "that into which" a thing is made) and everything is perfected by all that precedes and follows from its form. The form determines a being's *measurable* characteristics, "hence it is said that the measure marks the *mode*" (or particular manner of being).

The form itself is signified by the word *species*: "For everything is placed in its species by its form." (A form makes a thing the particular kind of thing it is.) *Number* refers to the measurable characteristics of the species, because definitions of species are like numbers, according to Aristotle: "For as a unit is added to, or taken from a number, changes its species, so a difference added to, or taken from a definition, changes its species."

So, we've addressed mode, measure, and number, but what of weight (not to mention rest and stability)? Thomas says that a thing's form follows an inclination to the proper end for that thing so that the thing acts in accordance with its form, which "belongs to weight and order." Achieving a proper end brings *rest* and *stability*.

To lighten the load of this weighty material, we might sum it up like this:

- Anything that actually exists is good in its *essence* (at the core of its nature or what it is) by the fact that it exists.

- Any physical thing that actually exists, is, in its essence, both *matter* and *form*, recalling that God (and angels, per Thomas) are form without matter.

- *Form* is that which makes a particular thing what it is, with measurable characteristics. (In a living thing, the form is the soul, which determines a living thing's growth and much more.)

- From a thing's form flows its *mode*, its manner of existing, like your own existence as a human being.

- A thing's *species* flows from its form, as the rational soul produces the human species, sensitive souls produce animal species, vegetative souls produce plant species, and inanimate (soulless) forms produce inanimate objects like minerals.

- *Number* refers to all of the measurable characteristics of the species, as we might describe, for a simple example, the mighty whale as seventy-nine feet long and the humble flea as about an eighth of an inch.

- *Weight* refers here not merely to the effects of gravity measurable by a scale; rather, weight and *order* describe a being's goal or end, the purpose for its being, and the place it can be said to rest when it attains its end.

- Therefore, everything that exists is good in its *mode*, *species*, and *order* (bearing in mind the relation of these terms to a thing's *essence*, *form*, *number*, and *weight* as well).

6   Is goodness rightly divided into the virtuous, the useful, and the pleasant?

This question was prompted by a division of goodness proposed by St. Ambrose (Augustine's mentor) in his ethics book *On Duties*. Thomas agrees that it is a proper division when speaking of *human goodness*.* Moreover, he believes that from a "higher and more universal view," the division applies to *goodness itself*. Everything that is good is desirable and serves as an end, satisfying an appetite once the good is obtained.

---

* Indeed, Thomas agreed with Aristotle in classifying human *friendships* according to those based on pleasure, utility, and virtue, a story I've told in The Four Friendships: From Aristotle to Aquinas (Brooklyn, NY: Angelico Press, 2018). "Four" friendships appear in the title because the book addresses not only how Thomas employed, adapted, and Christianized Aristotle's theory of friendship, but how St. Aelred of Rievaulx (1110-1167) did the same thing for Cicero's writings on friendship.

- Something that moves us toward a desirable end is good *relatively* in that it is *useful* as a means to satisfying our desires.

- Something that satisfies an appetite for the good *absolutely*, in and of itself, "is called the *virtuous*; for the virtuous is that which is desired for its own sake." (Virtue is its own reward.)

- Something that satisfies and terminates an appetite so that we *rest* in the thing desired is called *pleasant*. (To rest in the good is pleasurable.*)

Summa of Goodness in General

Goodness . . .

1 differs from being according to our perspective, but not in its fundamental reality.

2 is conceived in our intellect after we conceive being.

3 is found in every being.

4 acts as a final cause motivating actions.

5 consists in "mode, species, and order."

6 can be divided into the useful, the virtuous, and the pleasant.

---

* Thomas describes the process when he addresses the human passions (ST, I-II, Q. 22, a. 4). *Love* is our natural affinity for or inclination to good. *Desire* is our attraction to a good not yet attained. *Delight* or *joy* is our rest in the good we have attained.

6

GOD IS
GOOD

God alone is good essentially.

ST, I, Q. 6., a. 3

Now, having looked at good in general through Thomistic lenses, we are ready to peer more deeply into that childhood prayer and see what it means to say that "God is good."

1 *Is God good?*

It might appear that God cannot be good, because, as we've seen, goodness consists in mode, species, and order, but these don't apply to God. Further, although the good is what all things desire, all things do not desire God because not all things know him.

Thomas knows, however, that it is written: "The Lord is good for those who wait for him, to the soul that seeks him" (Lam. 3:25). Indeed, goodness belongs to God above all because a thing is good according to its desirableness. God is the font of all desirable goodness in all things. "Since God is the first effective cause of things, it is manifest that the aspects of good and of desirableness belong to him." As Dionysius puts it, God is called good "as by whom all things subsist" (maintain their existence).

Mode, species, and order pertain to the goodness of "caused good," created things, but "good is in God as its cause, and hence it belongs to him to impose mode, species, and order on others: wherefore these three things are in God as in their cause."

As for desiring God without knowing him, man, as a rational being, can "know him as he knows himself." Other creatures at the sensitive level of knowledge can know some participation in his goodness, and non-sentient beings have a natural desire without knowledge, "as being directed to their ends by a higher intelligence." (Perhaps here we can recall the fifth way from Q. 1, a. 3, in which Thomas concludes that "some intelligent being exists by whom all natural things are directed to their end; and this being we call God.")

2 Is God the supreme good?

It appears that the supreme good adds something to the good. Otherwise, every good would be the highest good. Everything added to something else is a compound, but we've seen that God is supremely simple (Q. 3, a. 7). Hence, God could not be the supreme good.

Thomas responds to this objection (and two others) by showing how God, though supremely simple, is indeed the supreme good. "God is the supreme good simply, and not only as existing in any genus or order of things." All perfections flow from God as the first cause, not as a univocal agent (as when a human causes another human, as we discussed in Q. 4, a. 2), but as a higher equivocal cause, which "is found more excellently, as heat is in the sun more excellently than it is in fire." Therefore, "as good is in God as in the first, but not univocal cause of all things, it must be in him in a most excellent way; and therefore he is called the supreme good."

As for the first objection in particular, the supreme good is not a composite. It "does not add to good any absolute thing, but only a relation." God is absolutely simple and good in himself. It is in our relation to him as creatures that we rightly call him the "supreme good," because we and "other things are deficient in comparison with it."

3   Does good in its essence belong to God alone?

We have seen that being and goodness differ in idea, but not in reality (Q. 5, a. 1). Some argued that everything that exists is good because of its own goodness, and therefore, everything is good essentially, according to its own nature.

Thomas begins his response with the words of Boethius in his *De Hebdomadibus* that "all things but God are good by participation," and not by their own essence. We, and all other existent things, have goodness because we share, in various ways, in the supreme goodness of God. "God alone is good essentially" (that is, by his nature).

Thomas says, "Everything is called good according to its perfection," and there is a threefold perfection:

A according to the constitution of a thing's own being,

B according to any accidents added as necessary for its perfect operation, and

C in attaining to something else as its end.

He elaborates that fire's first perfection is the existence it has through its substantial form as fire. Fire's second perfection consists of accidents such as heat, lightness, dryness, etc., and its third perfection "is to rest in its own place" and keep on burning.

This "triple perfection" belongs to no creature *by its own essence*, except for God, because:

A God's own being is the only being whose essence is existence (Q. 3, a. 4);

B There are no accidents in God (Q. 3, a. 6), "since whatever belongs to others accidentally belongs to him essentially; as, to be powerful, wise, in the like"; and

C God is not directed to anything else as an end, but is himself the final end of all things.

So we see that God alone is totally perfect by his own essence; "therefore, he alone is good essentially."

A twentieth-century commentator on the *Summa* sums it up nicely: "Creatures *have* goodness. God *is* goodness."[5]

4   *Are all good things good due to divine goodness?*

With that said, it might seem that all things are good "by the divine goodness," end of story. Perhaps surprisingly (at least it surprised me at first), Thomas argues against that idea:

> All things are good, inasmuch as they have being. But they are not called beings through divine being, but through their own being; therefore, all things are not good by the divine goodness, but by their own goodness.

Thomas's elaboration gets quite abstract and philosophical, weighing in on the differences in thought between Plato and Aristotle. But to answer the question succinctly, Thomas tells us that yes, everything can be called good from the divine good, which is "the first exemplary effective and final principle of goodness." Still, everything is deemed good "by reason of its similitude of the divine good, which is formally *its own goodness*." In sum, Thomas says, "So of all things there is one goodness, and yet many goodnesses." Indeed, the myriad of goodnesses in created things reflects, in an imperfect way, the ultimate goodness of the one Creator.

Summa of God's Goodness

God is . . .

1   good. "All things, by desiring their own perfection, desire God himself."

2   the supreme good and most excellent cause of all good.

3 the only being whose essence or nature is goodness itself.

4 the source and donor of the goodness that exists within every being as its own.

7

GOD IS
INFINITE

Things other than God be can
relatively infinite, but not absolutely infinite.

ST, I, Q. 7, a. 2

Thomas tells us that after considering "the divine perfection," we must move along to consider "the divine infinity"
(this chapter) and then "God's existence in things" (the stuff
of our next chapter). As a fan of professional arm-wrestling,
I'm aware and amused that one of the current greats in the
sport goes by the nickname "No Limits!" Well, we know
for a fact that the Blessed Mother herself told us of God,

"He has shown strength with his arm" (Luke 1:51). We'll examine God's strength and power when we get to chapter 25, but in this chapter, we will answer whether anyone, anything, or even God himself really has "no limits."

1 Is God infinite?

It might seem that God could not be infinite, lacking any kind of limitation, because, for example, the terms *finite* and *infinite* both refer to *quantity* (the amount of something), yet there can be no quantity in God, since he has no body (Q. 3, a. 1).

Thomas responds by citing St. John Damascene: "God is infinite and eternal, and boundless." He then notes that although ancient philosophers correctly saw that "things flow forth infinitely from the first principle," they erred in asserting that the first principle is matter. He elaborates (employing the "negative way") that we call a thing infinite because it is not finite. Next, he argues that "matter is in a way made finite by form, and the form by matter" and teases that out as follows:

- Before matter is made into a particular thing by its form, it is, in a way, infinite in terms of its potentiality to receive many kinds of forms. Once it receives a particular form, it is then limited to that form.

- Also, form is made finite by matter because form, considered by itself, "is common to many" (as humanity is common to me and all you reading along), but when the form is received into the matter (as the human soul is received into the matter of you or of me), the form is then determined to this one particular thing (or individual human being).

- Since matter is perfected by form, which makes it finite, infinity in matter "has the nature of something imperfect; for it is as it were formless matter."

- On the contrary, form is not perfected by matter, but is reduced or contracted, so, unlike matter, infinity in form "has the nature of something perfect."

- Recalling that being or existence is the "most formal" and perfect of all things (Q. 4, a. 1), and that the divine being (God) is not received into anything, but is his own self-subsistent being (Q. 4, a. 4), we must conclude that "God himself is infinite and perfect."

In response to the argument that God could not be of infinite quantity, Thomas replies that *quantity* is "terminated" (limited or rendered finite) by its form, even as mathematical figures are contained within their lines and surfaces. No material, bodily thing can be infinite in reality, since, having quantity, it will always be of some measurable size, and size is always finite. There could always be something bigger. Numbers have *potential* infinity because they can be infinitely multiplied or divided, but they cannot have *actual* infinity, which could not be added to or reduced. So, any theoretical infinity of quantity must be an infinity of matter, which, as we have seen, does not apply to God.

2 Can anything but God be infinite?

It would seem that things besides God could indeed be infinite. An infinite God would be *infinitely powerful*, so he could produce an *infinite effect*. Further, whatever is of infinite power is of *infinite essence*. Even our own *created intellects* have *infinite power* because we can apprehend universal principles that apply to "an infinitude of singular things." Therefore, it would seem that our created intellects are, in essence, infinite. Finally, primary matter is something different from God (Q. 3, a. 8), and it is infinite. Therefore, it seems, something other than God is infinite. (*Primary* or *prime matter* refers to pure materiality without any form—the raw potential for being, which does not actually exist until it receives a form that makes it some actual, particular thing, as Thomas will address at the end of his answer to this question.)

Thomas begins his response with a principle from Aristotle's *Physics* that "the infinite cannot have a beginning." Now, everything outside God came from God as its first principle. Clearly, then, God alone is infinite.

He elaborates that things besides God can be "relatively infinite, but not absolutely infinite." Consider the case of matter. Every material thing that actually exists has a form. In this sense, it is finite. Still, though every material thing has a *substantial* form that makes it the kind of thing it is, it remains in potentiality to many *accidental* forms. For example, wood is finite according to its substantial form as wood, but it is *relatively infinite* in that it retains the capacity to become an infinite number of shapes. Just ask any carpenter or woodworker!

So we can grant to actual material, bodily things an accidental, relative infinity of sorts, but no actual or absolute infinity.

Okay, but what about created forms that are not "received into" or combined with matter, but are actual and self-subsisting *as forms*? Some (including Thomas) think this is the case for angels—purely spiritual beings without bodily matter (though able to *assume* bodies to carry out specific missions for God). But even the angels, though existing as form and not rendered finite by matter, did not give themselves their own being. (God did that.) Therefore, their being has been "received into and contracted to a determinate (finite) nature," so even the angels are not absolutely infinite.

As for the counter-arguments we started with, regarding the idea that God, who is all-powerful, could create an infinite effect, Thomas notes that the essence of no created being can be its existence as it is for God, because *subsisting being*** is not *created being*. It is not in the nature of a created thing to be absolutely infinite. (And here is where things get very interesting, in your author's opinion!) Thomas explains that though God is indeed infinitely powerful, "he cannot make a thing made to be unmade." To do so would imply that two contradictory things are true at the same time. As we will examine further in chapter 16, God is truth, and he does not contradict it with falsity. "Therefore, he cannot make something to be absolutely infinite."

Regarding the power of the intellectual soul to extend itself to infinite things, this is possible because the intellect is a form not in matter, either *wholly separate* from matter (as is the case with the angels, explicated in I, Qs. 54-58), or *as an intellectual power,* "which is not the act of any organ, in the intellectual soul joined to a body" (as is the case with humans, and as explicated in I, Qs. 75-89). Such powers are given to intellects by God and, therefore, are not absolutely infinite of themselves.

---

* This is sometimes descried by the term *aseity,* which derives from the Latin *a* for "from" and *se* for "self." God is uncaused in that he is the first cause, needing no other cause for his existence. We might think back to the third proof from necessary being (Q. 2, a. 3) and to the great "I Am" of Exodus 3:14.

Finally, *primary matter* does not exist on its own in nature, since it is not actual, but only potential being. It is not created by itself, but must be *concreated* (created contemporaneously with something else) when it receives a form. Therefore, primary matter is only *relatively*, but not absolutely infinite.

3 Can an infinite magnitude exist?

It seems that infinite magnitudes can exist. Did not our high school geometry teachers start some demonstrations by stating, "Let this line be infinite"? Further, we know that "magnitude is infinitely divisible," because the definition of something as continuous is that it can be infinitely divided.* Since contrary principles are concerned about the same thing, and since "addition is opposed to division, and increase is opposed to diminution, it appears that magnitude can be increased to infinity."

Thomas responds to these and two other objections, starting with the declaration that every physical body has a surface and is finite because "surface is the term (*terminus* or limit) of a finite body." All bodies are therefore finite, and this applies both to surfaces and to lines.

He then makes a critical distinction that it is one thing

---

* A misunderstanding of this concept of infinitely divisible magnitude of distance led to some interesting paradoxes in ancient times, like Zeno of Ela's paradox of Achilles and the tortoise. It held that if a tortoise was given a head start in a race, even swift-footed Achilles could never catch him, for whenever Achilles reached the point at which the tortoise started or last reached, the tortoise would have moved some small distance farther ahead. Achilles would then have to breach that distance progressively, by, let's say, one quarter of the distance, then one half, on to the whole distance, and yet, by the time he did that, the tortoise would have moseyed his way yet a little farther!

to be infinite in *essence* and another thing to be infinite in *magnitude*. No created thing can be infinite in essence because its actual existence is limited when it receives the form that produces its actual existence. This would apply even to things like air and fire.

As for infinity in magnitude, Thomas says we can consider a body, which is a complete magnitude, either *mathematically*, regarding its *quantity* only, or *naturally*, regarding its *matter* and *form*. He lays this out as follows (in summary form):

- A natural body cannot be infinite because every natural body has a *substantial* form, which, as we've seen in the articles above, limits it, rendering it finite.

- Among the *accidents* of natural bodies is quantity, and since every natural body has a greater or smaller measurable quantity, it cannot be infinite.

- As regards *movement* of physical bodies, an infinite body could not have any natural movement because nothing moves unless it moves out of its place, and an infinite body would have no place it did not already reside in.

- Indeed, such a body could not move in an infinite *circle*, either, since that would require that one part of the body move to a place occupied by another part before, which would be impossible if the body were infinite in size.

- Even mathematical figures or bodies, if they actually existed, must possess some form, which would be finite, "for figure is confirmed by a term or boundary."

As for those high school geometry teachers, Thomas just says "geometricians." The geometrician does not have to assume an *actually* infinite line, but he takes some actually finite line, subtracts what he finds necessary (that is, its limits), and uses it for his demonstration. (Perhaps not completely unlike the "negative way.")

As for the idea that magnitude is infinitely divisible, Thomas replies that when we *divide* a whole, we "approach to matter," as a thing's parts are composed of matter, but when we *add*, we "approach to the whole which has the aspect of a form" (and a form, you will recall, limits matter). Therefore, the infinite is not in the addition of magnitude, but only in division." We can theoretically divide anything into infinite parts, but any whole thing that can be added to is not infinite.

4 Can an infinite multitude exist?

It might seem that there could be an infinite number of finite individual things, because, for example, it is possible for potentialities to be made actual, and numbers can be multiplied to infinity. Therefore, an infinite multitude of individual things could actually exist.

Thomas first responds with a scriptural verse we came across before (Q. 5, a. 5): "But thou hast arranged all things by measure and number and weight" (Wis. 11:20). This would indicate that no created thing could exist in an infinite multitude, which would be, by definition, without limits, unmeasurable, uncountable, unweighable.

Thomas notes that philosophers, such as the Arabs Avicenna and Algazel, held different opinions on this topic. Some held that an "actually infinite multitude" could exist, whereas others held that only an "accidentally infinite multitude" is possible. Thomas agrees with neither view, but posits that only a "potentially infinite multitude" is possible. At the risk of oversimplification, but to avoid further muddying of inherently murky metaphysical waters, let's bullet-point out and address each quantity in this variety of "infinite multitudes."

- Thomas holds that an "actually infinite multitude" could not possibly exist. It would require an infinite regress in causation. Something would be "dependent on an infinity for its existence; and hence its generation could never come to be because it is impossible to pass through an infinite medium."

- An "accidentally infinite multitude" could not exist, either. Thomas gives the example of what we might consider some immortal carpenter working without end and having from time to time to replace his broken hammers. The multitude of hammers that would arise over time would be accidental. That is, there would be no necessity for any particular number of hammers to be used to do his work. Only a few, or many, or an infinite number could be required, depending on how long they stay intact. Still, even such an accidental infinite multitude is not possible because "the species of multitude is reckoned by the species of numbers. But no species of number is infinite: for every number is multitude measured by one." Further, every natural multitude would come from the Creator, "and everything created is comprehended" by the Creator. As we saw in the passage from Wisdom, he knows their measure, number, and weight, which, therefore, could not be infinite.

- Nonetheless, Thomas holds that "a potentially infinite multitude is possible" in the sense that a number has potential infinity in that it can be endlessly multiplied or divided. As Msgr. Glenn clarifies, "an actual infinity is incapable of being multiplied or divided. What is actually infinite cannot be increased or diminished, but a number can always be added to or lessened."[6]

As for the opening argument that it is possible for potentialities to be made actual, Thomas notes that when any potentiality is made actual, it is done "according to its mode of being." For example, a day is not present all at once, but "is reduced to act" (made actual) successively (second by second). In the same way "the infinite in multitude is reduced to act successively, and not all at once; because every multitude can be succeeded by another multitude to infinity." No multitude of created things can be actual all at once.

Summa of God's Infinity

God is . . .

1 infinite, limitless, without beginning or end.

2 alone in absolute, actual infinity as self-subsistent being.

3 infinite as pure self-subsistent spirit, unlike any created thing that exists in a specific measure.

4 alone in absolute, actual infinity, unlike any merely potentially infinite multitude of things.

8

GOD
EXISTS
IN THINGS

God is in all things by his power,
inasmuch as all things are subject to his power;
he is by his presence in all things,
as all things are bare and open to his eyes;
he is in all things by his essence,
inasmuch as he is present to all
as the cause of their being.

ST, I, Q. 8, a. 3

God's infinity would seem to indicate that he is *omnipresent* (present everywhere), and indeed, even *in each and every thing*. In this chapter, St. Thomas determines if this is true, and what other truths God's omnipresence imply. Indeed, he will shed some light on just how in God "we live, and move, and have our being" (Acts. 17:28).

1 *Is God in all things?*

A Some argued that God could not be *in* all things because Scripture tells us he's *above* all things: "The Lord is high above all nations and his glory is above the heavens!" (Ps. 113 [112]:4).

B Others noted that what is *in* something is *contained* by it, but God rather *contains* other things and is not contained *in* them. Per Augustine in his *Eighty-Three Questions*, "In him things are, rather than he is in any place."

C Further, the more powerful something is, the greater its causal reach. Therefore, God can extend his action to things far removed from him.

D Finally, consider the demons. They are living things, but God is not in them, for "what fellowship has light with darkness?" (2 Cor. 6:14). Therefore, it seems that God is not in all things.

Thomas responds to the contrary that a thing is in whatever it controls or operates, and Scripture tells us God operates in all things: "Thou hast wrought for us all our works" (Isa. 26:12).

He then clarifies the particular way God exists in all things—not as their *essence*, nor as an *accident*, but "as an agent is present to that upon which it works." Aristotle demonstrated in his *Physics* that an agent must be joined to the thing upon which it acts immediately and touches by its power. In that sense, the thing moved and its mover are joined together. Well, since God is being by his essence, "created being must be his proper effect: as to ignite is the proper effect of fire." Just as light is caused in the air by the sun as long as the air remains illuminated, any being is caused by God and remains in existence by his ongoing power acting upon its inmost mode of being: being itself. (God, we could say, is in all things, not only as the Creator, but as their sustainer.) Further, "God is in all things, and innermostly."

As for the counter-arguments:

A Sure, God is *above* all things due to the excellence of his nature, but he is *in* all things as their creating and sustaining cause.

B That God does *contain* all things does not counter the fact that he is *in* all things. Physical beings are said to be *in* the things that contain them, but this does not apply to spiritual things, which contain the things in which they are "as the soul contains the body." (Consider that our spiritual soul does not sit there in any one part of the body, even the brain, but rather, it literally *animates* our entire body. It "ensouls it," giving life to it and enabling all of its powers.) So God, being purely spiritual, *contains* things: "Nevertheless by a similitude to corporeal things, it is said that all things are in God inasmuch as he contains them."

C As for the infinite reach of God's causal power, no matter how powerful an agent may be, it does not act "at a distance except through a medium." (Consider, for example, the modern electronic "medium" of *television*, which derives from Greek and Latin words meaning "to see from afar." We could not see televised images without the media of electronic signals within the video cameras far away, sent to an antenna and broadcast widely as microwaves, or sent out through coaxial cables, picked up by receivers within our home, and passed along to us, depending upon the messages *we* send to our TVs while sunk inside our sofas, clicking our remote controls. There are indeed many media involved in this powerful, far-reaching process.) God, however, does not require any media "middle men" and acts immediately in all things. Nothing then can be "afar" from God, because nothing can exist without God in it.

D As for those bothersome demons, as we noted before (Q. 5, a. 3) on the goodness in all things, even the demons, angels who rejected God, still have their nature, which is from God. Their "deformity of sin" came through their own free will and not from God. Therefore, we cannot properly say God is in demons without clarifying, "*inasmuch as they are beings.*" In things whose nature has not been deformed by sin, "we must say absolutely that God is [in them]."

2 Is God everywhere?

Are you old enough to remember the cartoon character Savoir-Faire from the 1960s? I just used another powerful medium to make sure I remembered him correctly (it's called the internet), and he's still there, all right! Anyway, this mischievous French–Canadian mouse would taunt his pursuer, Klondike Kat, with his heavily accented acclamation: "Savoir-Faire is everywhere!" Now, the mouse was clearly exaggerating, but could any being, even God himself, literally be *everywhere*? Let's ask Thomas.

Well, it's not looking good at the start. No less an authority than Boethius (*De Hebdomadibus*) wrote that "incorporeal things are not in a place," and to be everywhere means to be in every place. God has no body, and therefore, it seems, he cannot be everywhere. Consider too that what is completely in one place is not in another place. If God is in any place, he is "all in" (as we might say today). This is because we've seen that God has no parts (Q. 3, a. 7), so if he is in one place, there is no part of him to be somewhere else.

"On the contrary," says Thomas, quoting Jeremiah 23:24, "do not I fill heaven and earth, saith the Lord?"

God is in all things, as we have seen, "by giving them being, power, and operation; so he is in every place as giving it existence and locative power" (the capacity to exist as a particular place). God fills every place, but not like a body, which, when in a certain place, excludes the possibility of another body in the same place. When God is in a place, others are not excluded from it: "Indeed, by the very fact that he gives being to the things that fill every place, he himself fills every place."

The argument from Boethius does not apply to God's omnipresence because incorporeal, spiritual things are not in places "by contact of dimensive quantity, as bodies are, but by contact of power." (As we saw in our last section, lesser spiritual things, like the human soul, *contain* things, a body in our case, by their power.)

As for the idea that wherever God is, he is there wholly, since he has no parts, and could not be someplace else, Thomas clarifies by distinguishing *totality of quantity* from *totality of essence*. For any whole thing composed of parts, whenever that whole rests completely in any one place in the totality of its quantity (all of it), it cannot be in any other place, because the size of anything is identical to the size of the place that it fills. But totality of essence is not the same thing as totality of quantity. That which is whole by totality of essence in a thing can also be outside it.

Consider the example of some totally white thing. Whiteness is in that thing in terms of "totality of essence" because all of it is white. Whiteness is whole in each part of the thing's surface, because "its species" (whiteness) exists in every part of the surface. But if we consider the surface's quantity or size (an "accidental" form in contrast to its "essence" of whiteness), then the whiteness is not *whole* in every part of the surface. Still, this applies only to physical bodies. Spiritual bodies "have no totality either of themselves or accidentally, except in respect to the perfect idea of their essence. Hence, as the soul is whole in every part of the body, so is God whole in all things and in each one."

Truly, God can proclaim in any and all accents, "I AM is everywhere!"

3 Is God everywhere by essence, presence, and power?

He sure is, and in some profound ways. Rather than elaborate the four philosophically nuanced objections, we'll cut to the chase on this one and let Pope St. Gregory the Great (and then St. Thomas) spell this out in all its spellbinding magnificence.

In commenting on the Canticle of Canticles (Song of Solomon), chapter 5, Gregory says, "God by a common mode is in all things by his presence, power, and substance; still he is said to be present more familiarly in some by grace."

Thomas elaborates that God is *present* in a thing in two ways: as an efficient cause in all things he created and "as the object of operation is in the operator." This second way is most prominent in human beings, who have in the operations of our souls an implanted desire for God. (Recall Augustine's famous maxim that "our souls our restless until they rest in thee.") In this sense, "the thing known is in the one who knows, and the thing desired in the one desiring."

Things get interesting here as Thomas takes the Manicheans and a few others to task. The Manicheans (or Manichees) held that only spiritual, incorporeal things are subject to divine power, whereas visible, corporeal things are subject to the power of "a contrary principle."* Having seen that all created things come from God (Q. 2, a. 3) and are good (Q. 6), Thomas responds to the Manicheans that God is indeed in all things "by his power."

---

* Indeed, the spiritual realm was seen as a realm of goodness and light ruled by the Father of Light, whereas the material world was a realm of evil and darkness ruled by the King of Darkness. Augustine was a follower of this religion before he became Christian.

There were others who held that although all things are subject to divine power, God's providence does not extend to lower creatures. These people cited Job 22:14: "Thick clouds enwrap him so that he does not see, and he walks on the vault of heaven."

Though Thomas does not elaborate the point here, in his *Commentary on the Book of Job*, he notes that Eliphaz, who speaks those words to Job, refers to the erroneous view of some people that "because of the high character of his substance," God knows nothing but himself, since they think that knowledge of lower things would sully or defile his divine knowledge. Alternatively, others thought God knows things "universally, for example, by knowing the nature of their being or universal causes," but not as particular individuals.[7] Thomas says Eliphaz expresses these false views as believing that God cannot see us through thick clouds. Thomas believes that whereas *our* knowledge of God remains foggy or cloudy while here on earth, *God's* knowledge of all things is crystal-clear. God is indeed in *all* things, in every particular being in the universe, "by his essence."

Then there were still others who believed that though all things are subject to God's power, he did not directly create all things, but created the first creatures, who then created the creatures who followed. On the contrary, since God is the sole Creator, we must respond to these people that God is in all things "by his presence."

Thomas sums up in the powerful words that started this chapter:

> God is in all things by his power, inasmuch as all
> things are subject to his power; he is by his presence
> in all things, as all things are bare and open to his

eyes; he is in all things by his essence, inasmuch as he is present to all as the cause of their being.

He notes as well that God can also be present in humans according to his *grace* (which we will examine in chapter 12), and in "another special mode of God's existence in man by union."

4 Can God alone be everywhere?

Thomas lays out six carefully nuanced objections holding that beings other than God could be everywhere. Here, we'll zoom in on the first objection and then provide Thomas's definitive answer.

Some believed that "the Philosopher" (Aristotle) provided fodder for the view that things other than God could be omnipresent. Indeed, the category of the *universal* (as distinguished from the *particular*) "is everywhere and always." Further, since primary matter is in all bodies, it too is everywhere.

Thomas begins his rebuttal to all the objections with a powerful citation from St. Ambrose's book *On the Holy Spirit*: "Who dares to call the Holy Ghost a creature, who in all things, and everywhere, and always is, which assuredly belongs to divinity alone?"

Thomas answers that "to be everywhere primarily and absolutely is proper to God." In God alone can his whole self be present everywhere since he has no parts. What belongs to anything according to its *parts* does not belong to it *primarily*. For a simple example, "if a man has white teeth, whiteness belongs primarily not to the man but to his teeth." So whiteness is not in that man primarily. Now, God, having no parts, would be *wholly* in any number of places, "not as to part of him, but as to his very self." This would hold even were there an infinite number of places besides those that already exist, "for nothing can exist except by him."

As for arguments based on Aristotle, Thomas grants that the universal and primary matter is, in fact, everywhere, "but not according to the same mode of existence." Primary matter, you will recall, has *potential* existence, but not actual existence, until it receives a form. Thomas (and Aristotle, too) holds that universals are abstractions that describe what particular things share, as you and I share in the universal of human nature. *Humanity*, however, does not actually exist on its own outside you and me (not to mention everyone else).

God alone is everywhere. (Sorry, Monsieur Savoir-Faire!)

Summa of God's Existence in All Things

God is . . .

1 in all things.

2 in all places.

3 everywhere by his essence, presence, and power (and, in some souls, through grace and union).

4 the only omnipresent being, in light of being Being Itself and underlying everything that is.

9

GOD IS
CHANGELESS

God alone is altogether immutable, whereas
every other creature is in some way mutable.

ST, I, Q. 9, a. 2

Having seen that God is everywhere, all the time, Thomas
tells us we will next consider God's *immutability* (changeless-
ness) and his *eternity* (existence beyond time). This chapter
will be brief, addressing merely two articles.

1 *Is God completely unchangeable?*

Here are three reasons we might think God is *mutable*—that is, changeable:

> **A** Whatever moves itself is in some way mutable, in that it changes its place or position. Augustine says of God in his book on Genesis, "The Creator Spirit moves himself neither by time, nor by place." Since he "moves himself" in some way, he must be changeable.

> **B** Further, we know that God is wisdom itself, and Scripture tells us that "wisdom is more mobile than any motion" (Wis. 7:24). Therefore, God is movable.

> **C** To come closer and go farther away imply movement, and we read this in Scripture: "Draw near to God and he will draw near to you" (James 4:8). So God moves.

Thomas responds, to the contrary, with these clear words from Scripture: "For I the Lord do not change" (Mal. 3:6). He then provides a three-step logical argument, showing how what we have already learned in previous questions about what God is shows that he is immutable.

> **A** We saw that God is the first (and uncaused) being (Q. 2, a. 3). A first thing must be pure act without any mix of potentiality, because "potentiality is posterior to act." (That is, something that exists only potentially can come into existence only through the

causal power of something that already actually exists.) Everything that in any way changes has potentiality. Therefore, it is impossible for God to change. He has no unfulfilled potential to actualize.

B Everything that is changed or moved (Thomas uses the word *movetur*), stays as it was in part, and passes away in part. For example, if we were to paint a white object black, an accident of the object—its color—would change, but the substance of the object would remain the same. Our ability to see its whiteness would have passed away, but if we were to strip away the paint, our eyes would perceive the object in its original whiteness. So in everything that is moved, "there is some kind of composition to be found" (as in substance and accidents—recall that we saw in Q. 3, a. 6 that there are no accidental qualities in God).

C Everything that is changed acquires something it did not have before (for example, different color, size, density, place, knowledge, etc.). Now, as we saw in Qs. 4 and 8, God is perfect and infinite. He "comprehends in himself all the plentitude of perfection of all beings." Therefore, he cannot acquire anything he did not already have or move to any place where he was not already present. (Wherever he might go, he has already been there, and whatever perfections we might imagine acquiring, God's already "been there, done that.")

Of course, Thomas, being Thomas, also clarifies each of our opening objections one by one, yielding the last of this section's triad of threes:

A When Augustine says God "moves himself," he employs the philosophical language of Plato, who describes every *operation* as movement, "even as the acts of understanding, willing, and loving are called movements." Since God understands and loves himself, *in that sense*, he moves himself, but not in the sense of movement or change, which belongs to unfulfilled potentialities.

B Wisdom is described as highly mobile because of the way it spreads its likeness even to things farthest away. Indeed, everything that exists does so through its imitation, in some small way, of divine wisdom. Even at the human level, works of art flow from the wisdom of the artist. This simulates the way divine wisdom proceeds in degrees from the highest things, which participate more in its likeness (like man), to the lesser beings (like animals), which participate to a lesser extent. We call this a kind of "procession and movement of divine wisdom to things," much in the way we can say the sun proceeds to the earth because its rays touch the earth. As Dionysius wrote in his book *The Celestial Hierarchy*, "Every procession of the divine manifestation comes to us from the movement of the Father of Light." This is the kind of "movement" found in the divine wisdom of God.

© As for St. James's statement about God drawing near
to those who draw near to him, Thomas points out
that such things in Scripture are said of God metaphorically (as we addressed way back in Q. 1, a. 9).
Just as we talk about the sun entering a house as its
rays reach the house, so God is said to move toward
or away from us, depending on whether we decide to
"receive the influx of his goodness, or decline from
him."

2 Is God alone unchangeable?

This question should be of special interest to Catholics because two of the objections bring into play the nature of the
angels and the blessed human saints in heaven.

Some argued that things besides God could be immutable
because, as Aristotle noted, "matter is in everything which is
moved," but angels lack matter, and therefore cannot move.
Further, consider that everything that moves moves toward
some end or goal. The saints in heaven have already attained
their goal, so they must be immovable.

Thomas cites Augustine to the contrary (as he is wont to
do), who wrote in *On the Nature of the Good* that "God alone
is immutable; and whatever things he has made, being from
nothing, are mutable." Thomas then states clearly that "God
alone is altogether immutable; whereas, every creature is in
some way mutable."

Something that is changeable can be called so in two
ways: by *a power inside itself*, or by *a power possessed by another
outside it*.

Before they existed, all creatures were possible not
through the power of any created thing, but only through

God's causal power, since he alone could produce them into existence. Indeed, they remain in existence through his causal power as well: "Hence if he took away his action from them, all things would be reduced to nothing." Therefore, all created things are mutable because their existence or non-existence depends on the Creator's power.

As for changeability by *a power inside itself*, all created beings possess potentiality to change in some manner. This is readily seen in the corruptible things of earth, but it is even seen in the celestial bodies (like planets and stars), which some, based on the limited astronomical understanding of the day, believed were completely perfected and incorruptible by their form and could not undergo substantial change. Even granting that such created entities could exist and could not undergo substantial change, we see that they still retain the potentiality to move or change in place.

This also applies to the first objection regarding the angels. They are spiritual beings, lacking matter, and are immutable in terms of the substance of their being. They also have "immutability of election by divine power." (This refers to the fact that angels know what they know instantaneously, rather than through the step-by-step reasoning that humans employ. Further, when they exercise their will in making a choice, it is permanent and irrevocable. Hence, the angels who rejected God and joined with Satan can never change their will.) Still, the angels remain mutable in terms of *place*.

Now, most interestingly, I do not see that Thomas specifically addresses the objection citing the saints in heaven. Elsewhere in the *Summa*, however (Supplement, Qs. 82-85), Thomas elaborates on this passage from St. Paul: "What is sown is perishable, what is raised imperishable. It is sown in dishonor, it is raised in glory. It is sown in weakness, it is raised in power. It is sown a physical body, it is raised a spiritual body" (1 Cor. 15:42–44).

Thomas notes that after the resurrection, all human saints in heaven will change in that they will regain their bodies, but bodies glorified by God to possess impassibility (that is, to be imperishable), clarity (glory), agility (power), and subtlety (being like a spirit). Further, while our intellectual souls will bask in the unspeakable joy of the beatific vision of God's essence in heaven, God will give us far more powerful bodies so that we may move about to our souls' content through a glorified universe, including heaven and earth. So even the saints in heaven will be mutable and, in some ways, far more mobile than ever.

Summa of God's Immutability

God is . . .

1 as pure act, completely immutable (unchanging or unmoving).

2 alone in complete immutability.

10

GOD IS
ETERNAL

Words denoting different times
are applied to God, because his eternity
includes all times; not, as if he himself
were altered through present, past, and future.

ST, I, Q. 10, a. 2

Perhaps you recall Buzz Lightyear, the animated movie
hero, who proclaims, "To infinity and beyond!" It would
seem to be a play on words, since we saw in chapter 8 that
there is nothing beyond infinity, and God alone is infinite!
Still, if we look at the phrase in terms of what *topics* come

"beyond" (after) infinity as Thomas answers the question "What is God?", we'll see that omnipresence (existence everywhere and in everything) came next, followed by immutability (unchangeability). This brings us to the next topic "beyond infinity": eternity.

1 What is eternity?

Thomas begins his consideration of eternity by weighing the question of whether or not the definition Boethius gave in *The Consolation of Philosophy* is a good one: "Eternity is the simultaneously whole and perfect possession of interminable life."

Thomas provides six objections to potential flaws in this definition, and we'll address them all briefly (so it won't seem to take an eternity).

> **A** The word *interminable* is a negative term, meaning "without end." It should not appear in a definition of *eternity* because negation belongs only to what is *deficient* (recall that evil was defined as a lack of a good that ought to be present), but there is nothing lacking in eternity.

> **B** Eternity denotes a kind of duration, but duration relates to *existence* rather than *life*. Therefore, the word *existence* should replace "life" in the definition.

> **C** A whole is what has parts, but eternity has no parts, so the word *whole* should not be used.

> **D** Many days or times cannot occur together, all at once. "But in eternity days and times are in the plural, for

it is said: 'his going forth is from the beginning, from the days of eternity' (Mic. 5:2)." Therefore, the word *simultaneously* is incorrect.

E Moreover, the *whole* and the *perfect* are the same thing. To state both is redundant.

F Duration does not denote *possession*. Eternity relates to duration, not possession.

How interesting that these objections would strip the learned Boethius's definition of eternity of *every single word*. But Thomas concludes that the definition is indeed a good one! Let's see how.

Thomas begins by noting that we arise to our knowledge of unfamiliar simple things (like God's simplicity) through our knowledge of familiar compound things (that characterize all created things). We reach our understanding of *eternity* by means of our understanding of *time*. Time, Thomas tells us, "is nothing but the numbering of movement by *before* and *after*." Succession comes in every movement. One thing comes after another, through which we apprehend time (whether some movement or change is past, present, or future). Yet, for any simple thing without movement, which is always the same, there is no before or after. Our "apprehension of the uniformity of what is outside of movement, consists in the idea of eternity." Also, whereas changing things measured by time have beginnings and ends, whatever is unchangeable has no succession, no beginning, and no end.

In sum, then, eternity *is* properly known as what is "interminable" (without beginning or end), and as what lacks any succession, "being simultaneously whole."

As for our half-dozen (and, perhaps, half-baked?) objections:

A Simple things are usually described through negation, as we say that "a point is that which has no parts." This does not mean that the simple things we are describing are in some way deficient (recall the "negative way" of theology!), but rather that the intellect first apprehends compound things (because information is brought into our intellect through the data provided by our bodily senses), and then we derive our understanding of simple things through the mental process of abstraction, whereby we remove the accidental qualities of composites. For a simple example, when my eyes give me the image of my white, furry fifteen-pound American Eskimo Lily, and her "cousin" Randi, a seventy-pound Golden Retriever, my intellect is able (even at my age) to ignore their differences and abstract the essence they share of *canis lupus familiaris*. (Okay, *dog*.)

B Although it might seem obvious at first glance that eternity would relate more directly to the broader category of *existence*, rather than the narrower category of *life* (things that exist and also are alive), Thomas tells us that whatever is eternal not only is *being*, but must also be *living*. "Life extends to operation, which is not true of being." Time numbers the movement or change of any existing being that is not in a state of *operatio*—that is, a life of pure act or operation, without any potentiality, succession, or change.

C As for eternity lacking parts, that it does, but it is called whole not because of its combination of parts, but rather "because it is wanting in nothing."

D As for the "days of eternity" in Scripture, as God is often spoken of metaphorically in the Bible to aid our understanding, so too is eternity—"so eternity though simultaneously whole, is called by names implying time and succession."

E As for the ostensibly redundant use of the words *whole* and *perfect*, Thomas tells us both words are needed to distinguish eternity from time. Since time is successive, and the "now of time" is imperfect, the expression *simultaneously whole* is used to distinguish eternity from the *successiveness* of time, and the word *perfect* is used to distinguish eternity from the imperfect *now* of time.

F Finally, as regards the word *possession*, Thomas replies, "Whatever is possessed, is held firmly and quietly; therefore to designate the immutability and permanence of eternity, we use the word *possession*."

(We might imagine old Boethius smiling down upon Thomas from heaven as Thomas wrote this, our Angelic Doctor having restored every word of his attempt to define eternity!)

2 Is God eternal?

Hopefully, with a better understanding of just what eternity is and isn't, we can swiftly consider whether or not God is eternal. We'll cut to the chase with Thomas's answer and then see how he rebuts one of the more interesting objections.

Thomas begins by citing the Creed of St. Athanasius: "The Father is eternal, the Son is eternal, the Holy Ghost is eternal."

Moving on to the logical arguments, Thomas tells us, as we saw above, that the idea of eternity "flows from" the idea of immutability or unchangeableness. Since we saw that God is immutable, it follows the he is eternal as well. Indeed, Thomas tells us that not only is God eternal, but "he is his own eternity." No created being is its own being or its own duration. Since God is his own being and his own essence, "so he is his own eternity."

One of the most interesting arguments to the contrary cites two of the highest authorities in the realms of reason and faith. Aristotle wrote in his *Book of Causes** that God is "before eternity and he is after eternity," and we find in Exodus 15:18 that "the Lord shall reign for eternity and beyond" (sounding a bit like Buzz Lightyear, millennia before his time!).

Thomas replies, however, that God is said to be "before eternity," to mean "before it is shared by immaterial substances." The key idea there is the *sharing* of his eternity. Eternity itself "is nothing else but God himself." When the verse from Exodus describes God's reign as eternity "and beyond," this means beyond every age, beyond every kind of a duration measured by time. Indeed, as we read in the RSV-CE translation, "the Lord will reign for ever and ever."

---

* As noted before, not now believed to have actually been written by Aristotle.

3 Is God alone eternal?

It might seem that God's own words reveal that he is not the only eternal being. We read in Daniel 12:3 that some just people will be "as stars unto perpetual eternities."* Further, it is written: "Depart, ye cursed into eternal [Douay: everlasting] fire" (Matt. 25:41).

St. Jerome was well aware of these verses. Indeed, in a way, he "wrote the book" on them, as the translator of the Latin Vulgate edition of the Bible. Still, he notes that "God is the only one who has no beginning." Thomas reiterates the point we saw earlier that whatever has a beginning is not eternal. "Therefore, God is the only one eternal."

Again, eternity "truly and properly called" belongs to God alone, because eternity flows from immutability, and God alone is unchangeable. Sometimes Scripture refers to very old things as "eternal" metaphorically, like the "eternal hills" of Deuteronomy 33:12, but they are corruptible by nature. But God does choose to share his eternity with some creatures, such as the angels and saints in heaven, who are given everlasting life. As we read in John 17:3, "This is eternal life, that they know thee the only true God."

4 Does eternity differ from time?

Have you heard the phrase "the eternal now"? People with religious views from Protestantism to Zen Buddhism to New Ageism have given the phrase their unique interpretations. Here is a modern, generic first definition: "The

---

* The Dominican Fathers edition of the *Summa* notes that the Douay-Rheims translation uses "for all eternity" here. The RSV-CE uses "like the stars for ever and ever."

condition in which all reality is experienced in the present, with the past contained only in memory and the future only in anticipation or speculation."[8]

Now, going back a few thousand years, an objection notes that Aristotle wrote in his *Physics* that "the now of time" remains the same in the whole of time. Since the nature of eternity seems to be that "it is the same indivisible thing in the whole space of time," it would appear that "eternity is the now of time." Hence, "eternity is not different from time."

Thomas responds, however, that eternity as we've seen is "simultaneously whole," whereas time has a beginning and an end. Eternity and time are *not* the same thing. Still, the difference goes deeper than the differences in origins and endpoints. For even if, as some thought, the movements of the heavenly bodies had no beginning and will not end, the difference between eternity and time still holds for their case. Time applies to moving bodies, but eternity, as a "simultaneous whole," does not apply to bodies that move or change. Time is a measurement of movement, whereas "eternity is the measure of a permanent being."

Even though time always goes on, we can "consider the end and the beginning as potentialities." For example, we speak of the parts of time like the beginning of a day or year, but this cannot be applied to eternity, again, because of the fundamental essential difference, being that "eternity is simultaneously whole but time is not so."

As for Aristotle and the now of time, that now always refers to things that are changeable or movable, differing "in aspect as being here or there." So "the flow of the *now* as alternating in aspect, is time. But eternity remains the same according to both subject and aspect; and hence eternity is not the same as the *now* of time."

We might consider that in a certain sense, all we have on earth is, in fact, the *now*, in that the past is always behind us and the future always ahead of us, but it is hard to deny that our *now* truly flows and changes across time, rapidly becoming the past, and changing us right along with it. (If not, I'd like to have the same hairline I did when I was twenty.) We, and everything our eyes can see, are certainly far from immutable or eternal (though we can hope for eternal life one day if God shares this gift with us).

5 *What is aeviternity?*

Now, that's a good question. In my experience, *aeviternity* is a word that rarely comes up during casual conversations (okay, never). Thomas was addressing people who had heard of it, though, and his fifth article is entitled "The Difference of Aeviternity and Time."

Thomas starts his response again with the wisdom of Boethius, who wrote referring to God, "who commandest time to separate from aeviternity," thus positing a difference between time and aeviternity. Thomas continues, "Aeviternity differs from time, and from eternity, as the mean between both."

Here is one way of looking at it. Some say that whereas *eternity* has no beginning or end, and *time* has both beginning and end, *aeviternity* has a beginning but no end. Thomas says this is an "accidental" difference, however, and does not get to the heart of the true, substantial difference. He says that even *if* there were things in the universe that had no beginning and always existed with God, their *aeviternity* would still be different from both time and eternity. Let's try to make this as clear as we can.

The *Modern Latin-English Dictionary of St. Thomas Aquinas* notes the word *aevum* is "the measure of the duration of an incorruptible, and substantially immutable, but created being, i.e., an angel." Further, it is a synonym of *aeternitas participata*: "The eternity participated in and shared by the creature, the opposite of eternity of God." As for angels, Thomas says they "have an unchangeable being as regards their nature with changeableness as regards choice: moreover, they have changeableness of intelligence, of affections, and of places, in their own degree. Therefore, these are measured by *aeviternity*, which is a mean between eternity and time." Not even the incorruptible angels are truly *eternal*; only God is.

6   Is there only one aeviternity?

Here is perhaps a yet more esoteric question, but certainly worth a brief look. Some said for a variety of reasons that there are many different aeviternities. For example, consider that not all aeviternal things have the same duration. Some begin their existence after others. For an example that could not possibly hit closer to home, consider the case of *our individual souls*.

Thomas replies, "Aeviternity is a more simple thing than time, and is nearer to eternity. But time is one only. Therefore much more is aeverternity one only." He notes that there is "a twofold opinion" on the subject and dips into nuanced philosophical analysis of number and time before getting down to the "true reason why time is one." This "is to be found in the oneness of the first movement by which, since it is most simple, all other movements are measured." All other things derive their movement from this first movement and receive unity from it. Hence, time "is not multiplied by their multitude, because by one separate measure many things can be measured."

Even regarding spiritual substances, Thomas notes that there is another "twofold opinion" about whether or not there is more than one aeviternity. Thomas sides with the opinion that there is only one "because since each thing is measured by the most simple element of its genus, it must be that the existence of all aeviternal things should be measured by the existence of the first aeviternal thing, which is the more simple the nearer it is to the first." We find an elaboration in the aforementioned Latin-English dictionary: "Strictly speaking, there is only one *aevum*, the duration of the highest angel of spiritual substance."

As for our own souls, "all temporal things did not begin together; nevertheless there is one time for all of them, by reason of the first measured by time; and thus all aeviternal things have one aeviternity by reason of the first, though all did not being together." (I suppose we could say that although you and I may live in different time zones, strictly speaking, we share in one time—and in one aeviternity.)

Summa of God's Eternity

Eternity is . . .

1 "the simultaneously whole and perfect possession of interminable life."

God is . . .

2 eternal.

3 the only eternal being.

4 not limited by time, which has a before and after.

5 beyond aeviternity, for he has no beginning and does not merely participate in the eternity of any other.

Aeviternity is . . .

6 the mean between eternity and time, the eternity by which creatures participate and share in God's eternal life.

11

GOD IS
ONE

God is one in the supreme degree.

ST, I, Q. 12, a. 4

Next, we move, following Thomas from the celestial realm of the eternal God and aeviternal angels and saints to a no less philosophically fascinating, but perhaps more practically applicable, principle of the *unity* of God. Why not worship Zeus or Odin, Amun-Ra or Brahma, some might say, along with their fascinating pantheons? Well, in this chapter we will see how wide and unbridgeable the chasm between God and gods—as profound as the difference between *the one* and *the many*.

1 Does "one" add anything to being?

In addressing goodness in general and the goodness of God back in chapters 5 and 6, we started by considering whether *goodness* is really different from *being*. In this question preparing us to examine God's *unity*, Thomas asks "Whether One Adds Anything to Being?"

We'll address this question and the next one in brief, and then sink our mental teeth into the idea (and reality) of the oneness of God.

Some argued for various reasons (there are three objections)—for example, that one must add something to being, otherwise there would be no value in calling being *one* in addition to calling it *being*.

Thomas begins by citing Dionysius's *Divine Names*: "Nothing which exists is not in some way one." Thomas says this would be false if one were an addition to being, in the sense of limiting or further defining it. Hence, "*one* is not an addition to being."

Thomas explains that "*one* does not add any reality to *being*." It is only a negation of division, since *one* means an *undivided* being. This is why he says *one* is the same as *being*.

Every being is either simple or compound. Simple things are undivided, both in actuality and in potentiality. Compound things, to the contrary, do not possess their being while their parts are divided. (Consider for example, that without a soul the human body becomes merely a corpse.)

The being of anything demands that it be undivided, "hence it is that everything guards its unity as it guards its being." (Witness, for example, the drive for self-preservation within healthy living beings.)

As for the value in using separate words for *one* and *being*, this is appropriate because although one adds nothing to the *reality* of being, it does add an *idea* to being. (It gives us another way of thinking about being to understand it more deeply.)

2 Do "the one" and "the many" oppose each other?

Odd as it may seem, some argued that *one* and *many* are not mutually opposed, because, for example, nothing is made out of its opposite, yet a "multitude is constituted by one." (After all, we can count a multitude of things, one by one.) Further, we speak not of *one*, but of *few* as the opposite of *many*.

Thomas responds to the contrary that things that are opposed in idea are opposed to each other in reality as well. The idea of *one* is based on indivisibility, whereas the idea of *many* is based on divisibility. Therefore, *one* and *many* do oppose each other, indeed, in various ways. *One*, for example, is the principle of number, whereas *multitude* is number, "as the measure is to the thing measured."

As for the idea that nothing is constituted by its opposite, Thomas notes that *wholes* are "twofold," being either *homogenous* or *heterogenous*. Homogenous wholes are made up of the same parts, as every part of water is water, whereas heterogenous wholes are made up of dissimilar parts, as our bodies are made of bone, muscle, fat, etc.* In every heterog-

---

* Thomas again takes up the issue of homogenous and heterogenous wholes near the end of the *Summa* in the Supplement on the Resurrection, Q. 79, a. 3: "Is it necessary that the same ashes should return to the same parts in which they were before?" Short answer: Heterogenous parts will be arranged as before, but within homogenous parts, like bones, it would not change our identities as the selfsame person if there were differences in the arrangement of the tissue, since any differences would be accidental and not substantial. Still, he argues that for the sake of congruity, or fittingness, it seems likely that all of our parts will retain their original positions at the time of the resurrection.

enous whole, no single part possesses the form of the whole, as no heart or liver alone constitutes a man. Now, a *multitude* (i.e., the *many*) is this kind of heterogenous whole.

Consider too the example of the heterogenous whole of a house. A house is not built out of houses, but of various materials and structures. These materials and structures make up the house "by the fact that they are beings, not by the fact that they are not houses." In sum, heterogenous wholes are indeed, in a sense, composed of their opposites.

Oh, and as for *few*, rather than *one*, being the proper opposite to *many*—Thomas clarifies that *many* has a twofold sense as well. In the *absolute* sense, *many* is opposed to *one*, but in the sense of describing "some kind of excess," *many* is opposed to *few*. So, in the first, absolute sense, even two are properly considered many, but not in the second, relative sense.

3   Is God one?

Here is the question (and answer) we've been working toward. Perhaps surprisingly, the first of two objections to argue that God is *not one* cites Scripture: "Indeed, there are many gods and many lords" (1 Cor. 8:5). The second objection is metaphysical, arguing in part that since *one* is the principle of number (as we just saw in our last question), it cannot be predicated to (that is, it cannot apply to, or be a characteristic of) God, because quantity does not apply to God, who, as we've seen, is immaterial and spiritual (Q. 3, a. 1).

Thomas first counters with a pretty clear statement from Scripture: "Hear, O Israel, the Lord our God is one Lord" (Deut. 6:4).

He then lays out the logical argument "shown from these three sources."

A First, arguing from God's *simplicity* (Q. 3), Thomas tells us, "The reason why any particular thing is this particular thing is because it cannot be communicated to many." That Socrates (or you or I) is a *human being* can be communicated to many (for there are indeed many of us), but what makes us the *particular individual person* we are is communicable only to one. So if you, Socrates, or I were human because of what makes each of us an individual, there could not be many humans. This applies to God alone, "for God himself is his own nature" (Q. 3, a. 3). "Therefore, in the very same way, God is God, and he is this God. *Impossible is it therefore that many gods should exist.*"

B Secondly, arguing from *the infinity of God's perfection* (Q. 4, a. 2), Thomas reminds us that God contains within himself the whole perfection of being. If there were more than one God, the gods would have to differ from each other in some way, so something that belongs to one god would not belong to another. So if what was lacking in one were a privation or deficiency of some kind, then that god would not be absolutely perfect. On the other hand, if what was missing were a perfection, then one of them would lack it and be imperfect. "So it is impossible for many gods to exist." Even ancient Greek and Roman philosophers who lived in societies that embraced religions with pantheons, "constrained as it were by truth, when they asserted an infinite principle, asserted likewise that there was only one such principle." (Aristotle's Unmoved Mover, for example, was not simply Zeus, the father and leader of many gods, or Zeus's father, or Cronus's father.)

ℂ Thirdly, arguing from *the unity of the world*, Thomas says that all existing things are "ordered to each other since some serve others." Everything that exists serves a purpose and has its role to play. (Think of the modern concept of *ecosystems* and how biological organisms and even technological entities interact and influence one another within complex interconnected systems.) Recalling Thomas's fifth proof of God, the "argument from the governance of the world" (or from "final cause"), everything in the universe follows the laws of nature and achieves its goals as directed and ordered by the *one* supreme intelligence. That is to say, many diverse things are brought into order by *one*, "and this one is God."

As for the objections, St. Paul did *not* argue for the existence of many gods. (Indeed, in the RSV-CE of 1 Corinthians 8:5, "gods" and "lords" are put within quotation marks.) The passage describes the error of those who worshipped many gods as false idols. Hence, the apostle Paul adds, "Yet for us there is one God," etc.

As for one denoting a *quantity*, which cannot apply to a *spiritual* God, Thomas makes clear that *one* is "the principle of number" only for material things. This one belongs to the genus of mathematics, "which are material in being, and abstracted from matter in idea." The one of God is "one which is convertible with being," and is "a metaphysical entity," which does not depend on matter, in its being. God is indeed *one*, whole and indivisible, at the same time incorporeal and infinite.

4 *Is God supremely one?*

Granting that God is *one*, some argued that God is not *supremely* one (no more *one* than any other *one*). Perhaps the most interesting (and least technical) objection is pretty straightforward: "What is essentially good is supremely good. Therefore, what is essentially *one* is supremely *one*. But every being is essentially one, as the Philosopher (Aristotle) says" (*Metaphysics*, book 4).

Thomas starts his rebuttal with a statement from the great Cistercian St. Bernard of Clairvaux, who, in his work *On Consideration*, wrote, "Among all things called one, the unity of the divine Trinity holds the first place."

Now, it is later in the *Summa Theologica*, starting with Part I's Question 27, that Thomas shines his angelic intellect upon the mystery of the Holy Trinity—that the God who is one is also three persons. For now, our focus will remain on God's fundamental *unity*, or the *oneness* of the divine "three-ness," so to speak.

Thomas says that to be *one* is to be undivided, and if one being is *supremely* one, it must be both *supremely being* and *supremely undivided*. Both hold for God alone. He is supremely being because his being is not determined by any other nature to which it is joined, since God is "being itself, subsistent, absolutely undetermined." He is undivided because he is not divided any way whatever, actually or even potentially, since, as we've seen, he is completely simple (Q. 3, a. 7). Therefore, "God is *one* in the supreme degree."

As for the objection regarding supreme goodness and supreme oneness, Thomas replies that though every being is *one* by its substance ("it is what it is" by its substance, we might say), not every substance is an equal cause of unity; for the substance of some things is compound and of others simple. God, as we've seen, is utterly simple and supremely one.

Summa of God's Oneness

One is . . .

1   essentially the same as being, for everything that exists is the one thing that it is. (Though the *idea* of oneness adds to or enhances the *idea*, or our understanding, of being).

2   opposed to *many*, absolutely speaking, in that *one* means *indivisible*, whereas *many* is capable of division into numerable parts.

God is . . .

3   one, as seen through his simplicity, his infinity of perfection, and the unity of things in the world. (Indeed, the existence of more than one God is utterly impossible.)

4   uniquely and supremely one. His being is not joined with any other nature. He is completely indivisible as being itself, self-subsisting, and absolutely undetermined.

12

GOD IS
KNOWABLE

I answer that, since everything is
knowable according as it is actual, God, who is
pure act without any admixture of
potentiality, is in himself supremely knowable.

ST, I, Q. 12, a. 1

Next, we arrive at an interesting, important, and timely question: "How can we know God?" Pew Research interviews with Americans in 2018 and 2019 found that four percent described themselves as atheists and five percent as agnostics.[9] So a relative handful (though nine percent of the current U.S. population at that time would mean over 29 million people) believed they knew there is no God to know, or at least that *they* did not know whether or not God exists.

We addressed in chapter 3 the fundamentals of how reason can indeed show us that God exists. (In fact, he must!) We have also used reason (buttressed by revelation through Scripture) to learn some fascinating facts about what God isn't—and is, such as his simplicity, perfection, goodness, infinity, omnipresence, unchangeability, eternity, and unity.

In this chapter, Thomas tells us we are moving from the consideration "God is in himself . . . to consider in what manner he is in the knowledge of creatures."

Thomas, of course, is no agnostic. He knows well that God has provided ways for his creatures to know him. It's a fascinating but complicated topic. Indeed, Thomas addresses the subject in a full thirteen articles and forty objections and their replies. I suspect that you, dear reader, might object should I detail all of these. So, leaving objections aside for this chapter, we will cut, for the most part, to Thomas's bottom lines. If you'd like to examine all the lines that come before them, they are found in *ST*, I, Q. 12, "How God Is Known by Us."

1 Can any creature's intellect see the essence of God?

Yes. It is written: "We shall see him as he is" (1 John 3:2). This is because every knowable thing is not merely potential, but actual. God, who is pure act, without any potentiality, "is in himself supremely knowable."

It is true that what is supremely knowable in itself may not be knowable to a particular intellect, as is the case for the sun, a supremely visible object, that cannot be seen by bats because its light is excessive for them. For rational creatures, however, their ultimate perfection is found in heaven in the beatific vision of God, the principle of their being. All humans carry within us a natural desire to know the causes of any effects we observe, and this gives rise to wonder and awe. Nature does not operate without a purpose, and if intellects could not reach to the first cause, who is God, our natural desire would be in vain. When we read in the Gospels that "no one has ever seen God" (John 1:8), it refers not to the beatific vision, but the "vision of comprehension," meaning a perfect understanding of God (which we'll address more deeply in this chapter's seventh question).

2 Do we see the essence of God through an image?

No. When St. Paul wrote that "now we see in a mirror dimly, but then face to face" (1 Cor. 13:22), he meant that while here on earth we see God as reflected through the images of created things. (In his letter to the Romans [1:19], he wrote, "Ever since the creation of the world his invisible nature, namely his eternal power and deity, has been clearly perceived in the things that have been made.")

Thomas explains that two things are needed both for "sensible" and for "intellectual" vision: 1) the power of sight and 2) the union of the thing seen with the sight. Regarding material things, we see them not by union with their *essence*, but only by an image or *likeness*. When we see a rock, we do not get the substance of a rock in our eyes (thank God!), but only its form via the image produced by our visual power. Humans and rocks have different substances, each of which derives from God.

As for intellectual vision, God is the author of our intellectual power, and therefore, he can be seen by our intellect. Since my intellectual power and yours are certainly not the same as the essence of God, to see him requires some kind of "participated likeness of him who is the first intellect." Our intellectual powers are like an intelligible light derived from the first light, either in terms of our natural intellectual endowments or through some additional supernatural grace added by God. Still, even with super-added grace, we see "through a mirror dimly" on earth, because no created image or similitude can represent to us God's *essence*. As Dionysius wrote in *The Divine Names*, "By the similitudes of the inferior order of things, the superior can in no way be known to us." Thomas elucidates that "by the likeness of a body the essence of an incorporeal thing cannot be known."

To see God "face to face"—that is, not merely in reflection, but in his *essence*, as the angels and the saints in heaven do—requires the addition of God's gift to the blessed of "the light of glory" that strengthens the intellect to see God as he is. As we read in Scripture, "In thy light do we see light" (Ps. 36 [35]:10).

3 Can the bodily eye see the essence of God?

No. God cannot be seen by the sense of sight or any other bodily, sensitive power. These are all the acts of corporeal organs (as Thomas tells us he'll explain later in I, Q. 78). Now "act is proportional to the nature which possesses it." Corporeal, material powers, cannot reach beyond corporeal things (as we saw in the quote above from Dionysius). Therefore, we cannot see God through our physical eyes, or through images that build upon the data of any of our senses, "but only by the intellect."

We noted before that Thomas writes in the *Summa*'s Supplement on the Resurrection that we will receive perfected, glorified bodies. Even then, though, we will see God's essence not through our new, more powerful bodily eyes, but through our intellects, through "our mind's eye."* When a verse like Job 19:16 declares, "After my skin has been thus destroyed, then from my flesh I shall see God," it means not that we will see God with our fleshly eyes, but that when rejoined with the flesh in our glorified bodies, we will see God's essence with our "mind's eye." Let's see how Paul fleshes this out (if you'll pardon the pun): "May [God] give you a spirit of wisdom and of revelation in the knowledge of him" (Eph. 1:17).

4 Can created intellects see God's essence through their natural powers?

No. Even our "mind's eye" cannot see God's essence through our natural powers.

Thomas tells us the knowledge of every knower is determined by the knower's nature. If the "mode" or manner of existence of a being exceeds the mode of the knower, then knowledge of that object is above the nature of the knower and beyond its capacity.

Our souls possess two primary powers: 1) to know singular, material things through the power of our senses and 2) to abstract essences from individual things and know them as universal principles. This second power derives from the

---

* This reminds me of the story of first Soviet cosmonaut Yuri Gagarin, who, in 1961, was first to travel beyond earth's atmosphere. He was reported to have said (its veracity is disputed), "I went up to space, but I didn't encounter God." Certainly, Thomas would have been surprised if Gagarin had claimed he *did* see him!

power of the intellect, which itself is immaterial but is tied to our bodies during life on earth. Angelic intellects are not tied to matter, but not even angels are self-subsistent beings, as God is alone. So "to know self-subsistent being is natural to the divine intellect alone." God is above the nature of our created intellects. His essence exceeds our mental grasp, and even the grasp of the highest of angels. So created intellects cannot see God's essence by their own power, but they can if "God, by grace, unites himself to the created intellect, as an object made intelligible to it."

5 Does the created intellect need created light to see the essence of God?

Yes. Perhaps you'll recall from two sections ago Psalm 36 [35]: "In thy light do we see light." Thomas elaborates on our last question by explaining that for everything that exceeds its nature, the stage must be set by providing some disposition to receive what lies above its natural grasp. The increase of our intellectual power to see the essence of God is called "the illumination of the intellect." This light of glory is also mentioned in the book of Revelation (21:23) when describing the illumination of the city of God: "For the glory of God is its light."

6 Do some see God's essence more perfectly than others?

Yes. (And I will opine that this is an interesting question indeed, with important, personal, and everlasting implications for each of us.) We know that eternal life consists in the beatific vision of God: "This is eternal life, that they know thee the only true God," etc. (John 17:3). If we all saw God equally, all would be equal, but this contradicts what the apostle Paul told us: "Star differs from star in glory" (1 Cor. 15:41).

Thomas tells us that some of us will see God more clearly in heaven than others. And who might the clearest seers be? Those with more powerful eyesight? Or perhaps, more likely, the most intelligent people with the mightiest minds? No. And this is where our lesson becomes personally important.

We are enabled to see God in his essence through the light of glory, so whoever has more light of glory sees God more perfectly. And how do we get our unique measure of the light of glory? Well, in an important sense, it's up to us! It comes not through strength of body or power of mind, but *through how deeply we love God!* Thomas says that where there is more charity (love of God), there is more desire to see him, and our desire to see him prepares us to receive him as the object of desire. "Hence he who possesses the more charity will see God the more perfectly and will be more beatified."

Jesus told us to love God with all that we are. Those among us who accept God's gift of charity more fully will see the object of their love more clearly throughout eternity!

7 Do those who see God's essence comprehend him?

No. We read in Scripture, "O most mighty, great, and powerful, the Lord of hosts is thy name. Great in counsel and incomprehensible in thought" (Jer. 32:18, 19). Still, Augustine tells us that even "for the mind to attain to God in some degree is beatitude."

To *comprehend* means to know perfectly or completely. God is infinitely knowable, and no finite intellect could ever know him completely. Still, as Augustine has noted, any degree of knowledge of God in heaven will bring us bliss, and as Thomas noted just above, the more we allow God to inflame our hearts with charity while on earth, the more we will understand about him in heaven.

8 Do those who see God's essence see all in him?

No. Even the highest of angels who look upon God's essence do not know all things. Indeed, as Dionysius writes, the ignorance of lesser angels is cleared through the acts of superior angels.

Created intellects cannot see in God's essence all that God does or can do. We will see things in God as they are in him, "but all other things are in God as effects are in the power of their cause. Therefore, all things are seen in God as an effect is seen in its cause."

The more perfectly we can see a cause, the more perfectly we can see the effects that flow from it. For example, a person with a lofty understanding in some field can through the grasp of one fundamental principle draw many conclusions, but a person with less understanding or expertise will need specific examples and separate explanations. Still, we just saw that no created intellect can comprehend God through seeing his essence. Hence, no created intellect, human or angelic, can know all that God knows or does, "for this would be to comprehend his power." The more perfectly a created intellect sees God, the more it will know, but it will never know everything.

9 Do we see what is seen in God's essence through similitude?

No. In our second question, we found that we do not see God's *essence* through an image or similitude (that is, a likeness), but rather through the "light of glory." Here too, we find that those who see God's divine essence see what they see of *other things in God* not by images, but "by the divine essence itself united to their intellect." The details get abstract, but perhaps I can convey the gist of the idea by an analogy . . . though I must admit that it is way out there.

The first objection holds that "every kind of knowledge comes about by the knower being assimilated to the object known . . . as the eye by the similitude of color. Therefore, if the intellect of one who sees the divine essence understands any creatures in God, it must be informed by their similitudes." Thomas answers as follows: "The created intellect of one who sees God is assimilated to what is seen in God, inasmuch as it is united to the divine essence, in which the similitudes of all things pre-exist."

Here is where the way-out-there analogy comes in (if you'll forgive an author who has been watching too much science fiction lately). In the fictional series *Star Trek: Voyager*, the Borg are a species of cyborg creatures—humanoid life forms adapted with robotic and computerized parts. When they capture other species and convert them into the Borg, the process is called *assimilation*. (Those in the know will recall that "resistance is futile.") Assimilated beings, as the story goes, see and know things not according to the images of their own intellects, but through the hive mind. They all share in the vast knowledge of the entire collective. The

Borg lose their individuality and free will as they gain access to this store of knowledge, becoming essentially "drones."

Our analogy is that when we see things through God's essence, we do so not through the images of our individual intellects, but again, because we become united . . . not to the "hive," but "to the divine essence, in which the similitudes of all things pre-exist."

10 Do those who see God's essence see all they see in it at the same time?

Yes. Aristotle wrote in the *Topics* that "many things are known, but only one is understood," and Augustine wrote in his book on Genesis that "God moves the spiritual creatures according to time." These statements might suggest that humans in heaven, and even angels, see all they see in God's essence successively, not all at once. Thomas notes, to the contrary, that Augustine also writes, in his book on the Trinity, that "our thoughts will not be unstable, going to and fro one thing to another; but we shall see all we know at one glance."

Thomas says that what we see "in the Word" (in God's essence) is all seen at the same time. When many things can be understood by only one idea, they are understood at the same time. The parts of a whole are understood across time if considered in themselves, but when they are considered under the idea of the whole, they are all understood at once. We just saw that things seen in God are not seen individually according to their similitudes or images, "but all are seen by the one essence of God. Hence, they are seen simultaneously, and not successively."

As for Aristotle's statement, we understand one thing by

one idea, but many things can be understood by the same idea at the same time. For example, when we understand the idea of a man, we understand both "rational" and "animal," as when we understand the idea of a house, we understand walls and the roof at the same time. As for Augustine and the angels, they do not know all things simultaneously by their natural intellectual power, which still understands things successively, but what they see in God's essence is seen all at the same time.

11 Can any living person on earth see the essence of God?

No. (Or almost never, to be more precise.) The Lord said to Moses, "A man shall not see me and live" (Exod. 33:20). A medieval gloss on the verse says, "In this mortal life God can be seen by certain images, but not by the likeness itself of his own nature."* Thomas says a "mere" human being cannot see God in his essence, "except he be separated from mortal life." We saw in Question 4 that created intellects cannot see God through their natural powers because God's mode of existence (as self-subsistent being) surpasses their own. In an interesting aside, Thomas notes that "the more our soul is abstracted from corporeal things, the more it is capable of receiving abstract intelligible things." In dreams or in "alienations of the bodily senses" (like mystical visions and experiences), we are better able to perceive divine revelations and prophecies of future events. Only after our

---

* The *Glossa Ordinaria*, widely used in the Middle Ages, was a version of the Latin Vulgate Bible whose margins contained brief glosses (comments or explanations) compiled from the writings of various Church Fathers.

mortal life ends and our eternal life begins are we blessed with the light of glory and enabled to see God's essence, "face to face."

It is true that certain passages in Scripture seem to indicate otherwise. For example, Jacob says, "I have seen God face to face, and yet my life is persevered" (Gen. 33:20), and the Lord said of Moses, "With him I speak mouth to mouth, clearly, and not in dark speech, and he beholds the form of the Lord" (Num. 12:8). Thomas says Jacob speaks of seeing God through an imaginary vision of the type mentioned in the paragraph above, and which Thomas states he will explain further when examining the phenomenon of prophecy (II–II, Q. 174). Jacob "spoke thus to designate some exalted intellectual contemplation, above the ordinary state."

As for Moses, Thomas says God works *miracles* at times that do indeed enable living human beings to experience the vision of his essence. He agrees with Augustine, who wrote that God did this for Moses, "the teacher of the Jews," and for Paul, "the teacher of the Gentiles." (Thomas tells us he'll examine these miracles more deeply when he examines the question of "rapture" in II–II, Q. 175).

12 Can we know God while on earth through natural reason?

Yes and no (so to speak). As for the yes, Thomas shows in the second question of the *Summa* (and we saw in the second chapter in this book) that through natural reason, we can indeed know that God exists. There are no rational grounds for atheism or agnosticism. (We saw as well that the capacity to prove God's existence through reason is a dogma of the Catholic Church.)

As for the no, although reason, building upon the data of our senses, can tell us *that* God exists, it cannot completely grasp *what* God is. (This is why Thomas buttresses all of his answers with what has been revealed in Scripture.) Created things mirror God for us and point to him as Creator, as we read in Romans 1:19. Still, Thomas elaborates that "from knowledge of sensible things the whole power of God cannot be known: nor, therefore, can his essence be seen." In a Thomistic nutshell, "Reason cannot reach up to the simple form, so as to know *what it is*, but it can know *whether it is*."

13 Can grace provide us with a higher knowledge of God?

Yes. The apostle Paul says, "God has revealed to us through the Spirit . . . 'what no eye has seen, nor ear heard, nor the heart of man conceived'" (1 Cor. 2:10, 9). A gloss notes that this includes the philosophers (who stretched natural reason to its limits).

Thomas declares that we have a more perfect knowledge of God by grace than by natural reason. Knowledge derived from human reason contains two things: 1) images derived from sensible objects and 2) "the natural intelligible light"— that is, our intellectual powers of understanding, which enable us "to abstract from them intelligible conceptions," meaning to form universal concepts or ideas.

Now, grace perfects both things. The natural light of intellect "is strengthened by gratuitous light" when God showers us with his grace. Sometimes, too, even the images in the human imagination are "divinely formed, so as to express divine things better than those do which we receive from sensible objects." This may occur in the form of visible things, or even voices, to clearly express divine meaning. For example, when Jesus was baptized, the Holy Spirit was seen in the shape of a dove and the voice of God was *heard*: "This is my beloved Son, with whom I am well pleased" (Matt. 3:17).

Summa of God's Knowability by Creatures

God is . . .

1 seen in his essence by the blessed in heaven. (This is the beatific vision.)

2 not seen in his essence through the images or similitudes of any created intellect.

3 not seen in his essence with the bodily eye (even glorified bodily eyes in heaven).

4 not seen in his essence by any natural powers of any creature.

5 seen in his essence not by created light, but by the light of illumination or glory.

6 seen in his essence more clearly by beings who love him the most.

7 seen in his essence, but never fully comprehended by any creature.

8 seen in his essence, but the seer does not see all things in him.

9 such that, what things are seen in his essence are seen through his essence and not through images or similitudes within any creature.

10 such that, when seen in his essence or "Word," creatures see all that they see at the same time.

11 impossible for living creatures to see in his essence barring a miracle from him.

12 knowable by natural reason in *that* he exists, but not in *what* he is in his essence.

13 knowable in a manner exceeding natural reason through his supernatural grace.

(Grace perfects nature.)

GOD HAS
NAMES

The name God signifies the divine nature,
for this name was imposed to signify something
existing above all things, the principle
of all things and removed from all things; for those
who name God intend to signify all this.

ST, I, Q. 13, a. 8

After our consideration of the *divine knowledge*, St. Thomas moves next to the *divine names*, for we name everything based on what we know about it. In a dozen articles with thirty-eight objections and replies, Thomas dives into deep philosophical and theological waters—indeed, all the way into "the infinite ocean of substance." We'll cut short the details on the nautical search and focus on the treasures Thomas has uncovered for us, showing what it means to call God various names—including even to name him by the holy *Tetragrammaton*.

1   Can we give God a name?

Yes. It might seem otherwise to some. Dionysius wrote (perhaps ironically?) in *The Divine Names* that "'of him there is neither name, nor can one be found of him,' and it is written: 'what is his name, and what is the name of his Son, if thou knowest?' (Prov. 30:4)."

But Thomas notes that we read in Exodus 15:3 that "the Lord is a man of war; Almighty is his name." Moving from faith to reason, he informs us that according to Aristotle, "words are signs of ideas, and ideas the similitude of things." We use words to convey the meanings of things we conceive in our intellects. Therefore, we can apply a name to anything "as far as we can understand it." When we use the name *man*, for example, it expresses the essence of humanity. It signifies the definition of man by manifesting his essence (as rational animal). Therefore, the idea expressed by the word *man* is the definition.

We saw in the last chapter in Q. 11, aa. 11-12 that although we cannot understand the *essence* of God, we can see God as reflected in created things as their principle, though he is infinitely more excellent and remote from them. When Dionysius wrote that God has no name, or is above being named, he meant that God's *essence* "is above all that we understand about God and signify in word." We can apply names to God in accordance with the limitations through which we understand him, but we cannot define his essence.

2 *Can any name be applied to God's substance?*

Yes. Again, this may be counterintuitive to some. St. John Damascene wrote in *An Exposition of the Orthodox Faith*, "Everything said of God signifies not his substance, but rather shows forth what he is not: or expresses some relation, or something following from his nature or operation." (Here's another example of the use of the "negative way" of theology.)

Thomas counters with a statement from St. Augustine's *On the Trinity*: "The being of God is the being strong, or the being wise, or whatever else we may say of that simplicity whereby his substance is signified." Thomas tells us that the names of this kind, like *strong* and *wise* (Almighty or Wisdom), do indeed "signify the divine substance."

Names or descriptions of God that arise from negative theology (e.g., his simplicity, derived from his lack of any kind of composition), or that are based on his relation to creatures and emphasize the distance between them and him (e.g., creatures and Creator) do not apply to God's substance. Still, divine names like *strong* and *good* do signal God's substance, though imperfectly, as living creatures represent it imperfectly in themselves. (And here is where things get interesting.)

To say, "God is good" does not mean merely that he is not evil, or even that he is the cause of goodness, but that whatever good exists in any creature exists first in God, and in a higher, more excellent way. So God is good not because he causes goodness; rather, he causes goodness in things because he is good. As Augustine put it in *On Christian Doctrine*, "Because he is good, we are." So, yes. We can name God's substance (though imperfectly).

3 *Can any name in its literal sense be applied to God?*

Yes. We saw early on in Q. 1, aa. 9-10 that Holy Scripture uses metaphors as well as other literary senses, including the literal. The fact that we base our names for God on what we see in creatures might appear to limit us to metaphorical names, as when we compare him to a stone, a lion, and so on.

Thomas begins his discussion with a line from Ambrose's *Exposition of the Christian Faith* that mentions metaphorical description of the divinity—"by way of similitude"—but he also notes that some expressions regarding the divinity "express the clear truth of the divine majesty," which indicates that they describe God *literally*.

Thomas grants that our understanding of God does come from his perfections as they flow from him into creatures. Now, some names of creatures signify the *imperfect* way in which they reflect God, as the name *stone* signifies a purely material being (or *lion* signifies a being with sensitive but without rational powers). These kinds of names can be applied to God only in a metaphorical sense. Still, some names signify perfections *absolutely*, such as *being*, *good*, *living*, and similar names. In these cases, we can rightly say God is *literally* Being, Good, Life, etc.

4 Are the names of God synonymous?

No. If all the names of God meant the same thing, it would be redundant to use them. But, Thomas answers, they don't mean the same thing. He argues that such names do signify the divine substance, but imperfectly, and they do have different meanings.

Our ideas of God's perfection are formed from creatures that reflect in a myriad of ways what is united and simple within God. So, "to the various and multiplied conceptions of our intellect, there corresponds one simple principle, according to these conceptions, imperfectly understood."

To sum things up, all names that are applied to God signify one thing (God's substance), but "because they signify that under many and diverse aspects, they are not synonymous."

5 Do we say things about God and creatures in the same sense?

No. When something "is predicated of" (proclaimed or affirmed regarding) various things using the same name but not in the same sense, it is predicated *equivocally* rather than *univocally* (in the same sense). For example, if we say a man is wise, we refer to a quality belonging to the man distinct from his essence of humanity or from his existence, but wisdom is not one of a number of qualities belonging to God distinct from his essence and existence. Any kind of perfection we refer to in a creature signifies that perfection distinct in idea from other perfections, none of which captures the perfection in the full degree in which it flows undivided from God, its cause.

This is not to say that names applied to God and creatures are purely equivocal and demonstrate nothing at all about God. Let's revisit what St. Paul told us: "His invisible nature, namely his eternal power and deity, has been clearly perceived in the things that have been made" (Rom. 1:20). Names applied to God and creatures are used "in an analogous sense, that is, according to proportion." In *analogies*, the ideas are not univocal, meaning the same thing, but neither are they totally different, either. In a way, analogies are a mean or middle ground between "pure equivocation and simple univocation." (Analogies applied to God and creatures are not complete in their meaning, but neither are they empty.)

6 Do the names given God apply primarily to creatures?

No, yet it may seem so, since, as Aristotle notes, names are signs of ideas, and our ideas spring from our senses that detect created things. Further, Dionysius notes, "We name God from creatures."

Thomas first counters from Scripture: "I bow my knees before the Father, from whom every family in heaven and on earth is named" (Eph. 3:14-15).

Names applied to things in the analogical sense (as we discussed above pertaining to God and creatures) all refer "to some one thing; and this one thing must be placed in the definition of them all." Now, when we use metaphorical names for God, the names are applied to creatures primarily, because when used to name God, they point only to similarities with those creatures (as when we used the examples of *stone* or *lion* a couple of questions back). Thomas gives another rather poetic example here. When we say a field is "smiling," we mean that the beauty of its flowering is like the beauty of a person's smile "by proportionate likeness." So the name *lion* applied to God means only that God manifests strength in his works, as lions do.*

Other names of God do not apply primarily to creatures, however. We saw before that to say God is good or wise is not only to say he causes goodness or wisdom in creatures, "but that these exist in him in a more excellent way." Therefore, in terms of *what such names signify*, they refer primarily to God and only secondarily to creatures, "because these perfections flow from God to creatures." In terms of *"the imposition of the names"* (how we go about generating and applying the names), as Aristotle noted, they are first applied by us to creatures, because we know the creatures first. As for Dionysius's statement, he means we derive merely metaphorical names primarily from creatures.

7 Do names that imply relation to creatures apply to God across time as opposed to eternity?

Admittedly, this one is a bit of a doozy at first glance. To cut through six perhaps esoteric objections and get to the bottom line, Thomas agrees with Augustine, who wrote "that this relative appellation *Lord* is applied temporally." Any names of God that derive from his relation to creatures "are applied to God temporally, and not from eternity." So, in short: yes.

---

* My thoughts always go to the lion Aslan in C. S. Lewis's *Chronicles of Narnia*, symbolizing Jesus Christ by the lion's kingliness and as "the Lion of tribe of Judah" (Rev. 5:5).

In other words, such names, though still meaningful, do not signify God's *essence*, which is *eternal*, but describe his relationship with creatures whom he invented *in time*. The name *Lord*, for instance, includes the idea of a servant and vice versa. These two relative terms are simultaneous in nature. To use one implies the other. Therefore, God could not be appropriately called *Lord* (as the Lord over all creation) until he made creatures subject to himself. Other important but temporal names for God include *Creator* and *Savior*, which appropriately address God in *temporal* terms in relation to his creatures but do not address his *eternal* essence.

Indeed, to believe in God *only* in terms of his temporal names opens the door to a variety of heresies. Consider, for example, the Arians of the third and fourth centuries, who saw Jesus Christ as savior but considered him a created, temporal being, declaring that "there was a time when he was not."* The Arians thus denied the eternity, omnipotence, and more entailed in his name of *Word*, as made clear in the first verse of John's Gospel: "In the beginning was the Word, and the Word was with God, and the Word was God."

8 *Does the name "God" apply to God's nature?*

Yes. Whereas St. Ambrose states this as clearly as could be— "God is a name of the nature"—Thomas uses some subtlety. We name some things according to their operations or property. To use a modern example that we employed in a different context in Q. 8, a. 1, the *television* was named

---

* For more details on Arianism, see Kenneth D. Whitehead, "The Heresies that Just Won't Go Away," *Catholic Answers Magazine*, Feb. 1, 2006, https://www.catholic.com/magazine/print-edition/they-just-wont-go-away.

from its *operation*, in that it lets us see (Latin, *visio*) from afar (Greek, *tele*). Though our televisions certainly do just that, when we use the word *television*, we refer to the *substance* of that box or screen sitting on the console or mounted to the wall that allows us to see those images from afar. Other things are named directly as they are known to us in themselves (in their substance), such as "heat," "cold," "whiteness," and so forth. For such things the meaning and the source of the name are the same.

Since we cannot know God directly in his nature, but we come to know him through his operations or effects, we can indeed name him through those. Therefore, the name *God* does arrive through his operation or acts (as was the case for our example of a television). The name *God* is applied "from his universal providence over all things." (Quite an operation, no?) When we use the name *God*, we intend to name him who exercises providence over all things. (We'll examine God's providence in detail in chapter 22.) As Dionysius wrote, "The deity watches over all with perfect providence."

Although the name *God* is taken from operation, it signifies the divine nature. Thomas sums things up as follows: "Thus the name *God* signifies divine nature, for this name was imposed to signify something existing above all things, the principle of all things and removed from all things; for those who name God intend to signify all this."

9 *Is the name* God *communicable?*

The answer is *no*, but first we should be sure we understand the question! Thomas is asking if the name *God* can also be applied to other things besides God. As for scriptural texts that seem to imply that it can, consider 2 Peter 1:4: "He has granted us his precious and very great promises, that through these you may escape from corruption . . . and become partakers of divine nature," and Psalm 82 [81]:6: "I say, 'You are gods.'" Further, we just saw that the name *God* comes from his operation or effects, but these are communicable, as when we call a person *good* or *wise*. So why would not the name God be communicable, too?

To root his response in Scripture, Thomas cites Wisdom 14:21, in its reference to the divine name: "Men, in bondage to misfortune or to royal authority, bestowed on objects of stone or wood that name that ought not to be shared." The name *God* is not communicable. It is not to be given to any creature.

Thomas elaborates that a name can be communicable in two senses: 1) by similitude, and 2) properly. Individual things can be named according to similarity, as we might call a strong man *Achilles* because he is strong and brave like Achilles, but we are speaking metaphorically. Our strong, brave man shares some of the many properties of the legendary Achilles. God, however, refers not to an individual, composed of body and soul, and possessing various properties, but to self-subsistent being. Further, as we saw in Q. 11, a. 3, since divine nature cannot be multiplied, the name of God is incommunicable in reality (or properly speaking).

Psalm 82 [81]'s "you are gods" refers to people who are called gods by similitude, who share in some way in the divinity by likeness. We are called to be *partakers in* the divine nature but not to become the divine nature. As for names like *good* and *wise* that we may share with God, these derive from the perfections that proceed from God to creatures and do not signify the divine nature and its absolute perfections in themselves. In short, properly speaking, the name *God* belongs to God alone.

10 *In what sense is the name* God *applied to God?*

This question is another doozy. Thomas's original title is as follows: "Whether This Name, 'God,' Is Applied to God Univocally by Nature, by Participation, and According to Opinion?" It is also an interesting question, because Thomas specifically references the understanding of "Catholicus" (a Catholic), in contrast to that of a pagan.

When a pagan says that some idol or graven image is *God*, he does not refer to the true deity, because "no one can signify what he does not know," and "the heathen does not know the divine nature." The heathen applies the name *God* only *equivocally* and according to his *opinion* (which is wrong, divorced from reality). It is equivocal in the manner of applying the word *animal* to a picture of an animal rather than the true animal. "On the other hand, a Catholic signifies the true deity when he says there is one God."

Thomas elaborates that a true idea of God (as we have been fleshing out, so to speak, in chapter after chapter) "includes the idea of God when it is used to denote God in opinion, or participation. For when we name anyone *God* by participation, we understand by the name of *God* some likeness of the true God." In a similar way, if we call an idol *God*, we mean that it signifies something that some people *think* is God (a matter of false opinion). Again, we do not speak of God *univocally* (with terms meaning exactly the same thing) because we do not know God's essence. What we appropriately say of God is said by way of *analogy* (through relevant similarities between the partial perfections of created things and the absolute perfection of the Creator).

11 *Is* He Who Is *God's most proper name?*

Yes. This is a fascinating question that spells out the meaning of the name God divulged to Moses when Moses asked him what name Moses should give when the people ask who sent him: "Thou shalt say to them He Who Is hath sent me to you" (Exod. 3:13-14). In Thomas's Latin, this name is *Qui Est*, and Thomas concludes that *He Who Is* "is most properly applied to God." He gives three reasons:

A Because of its *signification*. It does not refer to *form*, but simply to *existence* itself. We saw before (Q. 3, a. 4) that God's *existence* and *essence* are one, which can be said of no other. So *Qui Est*, above all other names, refers to God alone, for everything else is named according to its form.

B Because of its *universality*. All other names are less universal, adding something in particular, even if only in idea. Since we cannot know God's essence in this life, whatever mode we use to express our understanding of God "falls short of the mode of God himself." Therefore, the less determinate and more universal and absolute they are, the more appropriate names are to God. As John Damascene said quite elegantly, "*He Who Is* is the principal of all names applied to God; for comprehending all in itself, it contains existence itself as an infinite and indeterminate sea of substance." Thomas elaborates that *He Who Is* specifies no particular mode of being, but denominates "the infinite ocean of substance."

C Because of its *cosignification*. It uses the present state to signify present existence, since in God's eternal now there is no past or future.

If I might conclude on a personal note, one of my favorite old tee-shirts depicts the cartoon sailor Popeye and one of his best known sayings: "I yam what I yam." Any one of us can truly declare, "I am what I am." God alone can chop off the last three words and declare simply, "I Am."

12 Can we make affirmative statements about God?

Yes. We are not limited entirely to the negations of negative theology when it comes to forming true statements about God. True, Dionysius wrote in *The Celestial Hierarchy* that "negations about God are true, but affirmations are vague." Further, Boethius wrote in *On the Trinity* that "a simple form cannot be a subject." Still, Thomas responds, "What is of faith cannot be false," and many affirmative propositions (positive statements) are made about God. These include "that God is three and one: and that he is omnipotent." Therefore, true affirmative statements can indeed be made about God.

If you'll hang with me here for a minute, we must consider "that in every true affirmative proposition the predicate and the subject signify in some way the same thing in reality, and different things in idea." To make this simple, *man* and *white* are the same in subject and different in idea in referring to a white man. When we say *man is an animal*, the same applies because the same thing that is man is truly animal, too. In the same *suppositum* (individual substance) "there is sensible nature by reason of which he is called animal, and the rational nature by which he is called man." So the predicate and subject are the same in substance but different in idea.

God, however, is not a *suppositum*, but is one and simple. Our intellect knows him by different ideas because we cannot see him as he is in himself. Still, we understand him through different conceptions or ideas, and we know that "one and the same simple object corresponds" to these conceptions. "Therefore the plurality of predicate and subject represents the plurality of idea; and the intellect represents the unity by composition." (In a sense, we might say that the best we can do through human *reason* is to piece together our affirmative conceptions of the one God through many different ideas within our ken. *Faith* then surpasses the limits of our reason through what God reveals to us.)

As for our good friends and guides, Dionysius and Boethius, when Dionysius says affirmative statements about God are vague (or "incongruous" in one translation), he means that "no name can be applied to God according to its mode of signification" (which exceeds the powers of any created intellect). As for Boethius, who stated that simple forms cannot be subjects of our affirmative statements, Thomas notes that although our intellects cannot comprehend simple subsisting forms as they are in themselves, we do apprehend the forms within compound things, wherein something is taken as the subject (like a particular man) and something else as a predicate inherent in the subject (that he is white or an animal, for example). Therefore, the intellect "apprehends the simple form as a subject, and attributes something else to it. We cannot see humanity, but we can see individual men and women, and make affirmative statements about them." So, though God, as we saw (Q. 3), is pure form, we can still make affirmative statements about him.

Summa of the Names of God

God . . .

1 is fittingly given names by his creatures.

2 can be named in his substance (as *Good* or *Wise*, for example), in an imperfect way.

3 can be named literally (with words like *being*, *good*, and *living*).

4 can be given multiple names that are not synonymous or redundant, since they signify the one thing of God under many and different aspects.

5 is named equivocally and analogously by names that represent multiple and divided perfections existing in creatures that pre-exist unitedly in God.

6 is known to us through creatures, but the names of God refer primarily to him rather than to creatures, because the perfections we see in creatures flow from God to them.

7 is known by some names that are temporal (time-based), rather than reflecting his eternity, because these names (like *Lord*, *Creator*, and *Savior*) depend upon his

relationships with beings that exist in time after he created them.

8 when named *God*, is named according to his nature exercising divine Providence over all things.

9 is the name for God alone, and cannot be shared by any other.

10 when named by Catholics, signifies the true deity, but not when named by heathens, since they do not know the divine nature (and will often have multiple gods or idols).

11 is most properly named "HE WHO IS," as he revealed in Scripture (Exod. 3:14)—he whose essence and existence are one, he who is the "infinite ocean of substance," he who is eternally present, without past or future.

12 can be named and described through affirmative statements, as is clear through fundamental revealed truths (e.g., the Trinity, God's omnipotence), and through the fact that our intellects were crafted to rise to immaterial truths through the powers of our senses.

PART IV

WHAT DOES GOD
KNOW?

Now the power of God in his knowing is
as great as his actuality in existing.

ST, I, Q. 14, a. 3

14

GOD'S
KNOWLEDGE

I answer that in God there
exists the most perfect knowledge.

ST, I, Q. 14, a. 1

St. Thomas tells us that after having considered God's substance in the previous questions, "we have now to treat of God's operation." In a sense, we are moving from the question "What is God?" to the questions "What does God know?" and "What does God do?" As for "operation," some acts are *immanent*, taking place within an agent, and other operations produce *exterior* effects. First up, we will examine the immanent operations of God's *intelligence* and *will*, and then we will move on to the exterior operations manifesting God's *power*. In this chapter we zoom in on the immanent intellectual operation of God's *knowledge*. Keeping in mind that Thomas addresses the topic with sixteen questions containing over forty objections, for most questions after the first one to set the stage, we'll cut to the chase in pithy summaries of Thomas's answers.

1 *Is there knowledge in God?*

Yes . . . and we might add, "Of course!" People typically speak of God as *omniscient* (all-knowing), so to ask if he has knowledge may seem silly.

Thomas refers to *scientia* (knowledge in our translation) as the name of one of three *intellectual virtues* of *science* (or *knowledge*), *understanding*, and *wisdom*. Aristotle wrote about them in his *Nicomachean Ethics*, and Thomas fleshes them out later in ST, I-II, Q. 57. Further, you can find them all together in Scripture. For example, "For the Lord gives wisdom; from his mouth come knowledge and understanding" (Prov. 2:6) and "By wisdom a house is built, and by understanding it is established, by knowledge its rooms are filled with all pleasant and precious riches" (Prov. 24:3-4).

Here is one reason why our question about God's knowledge arises. The virtue of *science* or *knowledge* (through which we grasp cause-and-effect relationships) exists within us as a *habit*, since all virtues are habits, or dispositions that we build within ourselves. Habits can be seen as *means* or midway points between *potentiality* and *act*. For example, in the case of *fortitude* or courage, we all have the potential to develop it in ourselves, and if we have done so, we are more likely to engage in actual courageous acts than a person who has not developed that virtue. But, as we have seen time and again, there is no potential in God, since he is pure act. Therefore, it does not make sense to say science or knowledge (a middle point between potentiality and act) is in him.

Now let's get to the heart of the answer. Scripture clearly speaks of God's knowledge: "O the depth of the riches and wisdom and knowledge of God" (Rom. 11:33). In fact, the most perfect of all knowledge is in God. We can see this through the hierarchy of knowledge. Beings without intelligence possess only their own forms, whereas intelligent beings are adapted to receive the forms of other beings. So the nature of non-intelligent beings is far more cramped and limited than the greater reach and power of intelligent beings. In *On the Soul*, Aristotle said that "the soul is in a sense all things." A human intellectual soul can acquire knowledge by receiving the forms of all sorts of things, from insects to galaxies, without having to take in their matter (since we would run out of space in our bodies quickly in the case of things like galaxies). Rather, the intellectual soul can take in diverse forms because it is *immaterial*.

The immateriality of a thing is what makes it *cognitive* (capable of knowing other forms). Plants know nothing, because they are wholly material. *Sensation*, however, is cognitive, because it can receive images without the matter (for example, as animals can see stones without getting stones in their eyes), and the human *intellect* is even more cognitive because it is separate and unmixed with matter (as when we conceive of universal concepts not tied to any particular things). The intellect most immaterial of all is God's. Therefore, "he occupies the highest place in knowledge."

As for the habit or virtue of science or knowledge, as

Proverbs 2:6 makes clear, intellectual virtues, including knowledge, come to us through God. We receive such perfections from him according to our own imperfect manner of existence. They exist in us in an imperfect way as virtuous habits between potentiality and act. They exist in God perfectly, not as a habit, but as "substance and pure act."

2 Does God understand himself?

Yes. Some argued, building on Augustine, that "our intellect understands itself, only as it understands other things" and believed that this must apply to God as well. Scripture tells us, however, "No one comprehends the thoughts of God except the Spirit of God" (1 Cor. 2:11).

Our acts of understanding depend upon receiving the forms of things outside ourselves. We come to feel or know things when our intellect or sense is informed or acted upon by *sensible species* (the images we build based upon what we perceive through our sense, like a *particular* dog) or *intelligible species* (the concepts we construct from the abstractions produced by our intellect, like the entire *species* of animal we classify as *dog*). Hence, our sense or intellect is separate and distinct from sensible or intelligible objects, and is therefore in a state of potentiality.

God has no potentiality, being pure act, so "his intellect and its object are altogether the same." He is never without intelligible species, nor do intelligible things differ from the substance of his divine intellect. "The intelligible species of God is the divine intellect itself, and thus God understands himself through himself." (God, unlike us, need not look outside his self to understand his self.)

3 *Does God comprehend himself?*

Yes. Augustine wrote that "everything that understands itself comprehends itself." Thomas adds, "But God understands himself. Therefore, he comprehends himself."

Comprehension refers to knowing something "as perfectly as it is knowable." God knows himself as perfectly as he is perfectly knowable. Aristotle notes in the *Metaphysics* that everything known is known according to its actuality, "since a thing is not known in potentiality." (We know things not as they might be, but as they are.) As for God, "the power of God in knowing is as great as his actuality in existing; because it is from the fact that he is in act and free from all matter and potentiality, that God is cognitive . . . whence it is manifest that he knows himself as much as he is knowable, and for that reason he perfectly knows himself."

4 *Is the act of God's intellect his substance?*

Yes. Augustine wrote in *On the Trinity*, "In God, to be is the same as to be wise." Thomas elaborates that to be wise is the same as to understand, so in God, to be is the same as to understand, because, as we saw in Q. 3, a. 4, God's existence is his essence or substance. "Therefore, the act of God's intellect is his substance."

Moreover, Thomas adds (with awe-inspiring insight) that we can conclude from what we have considered thus far that "in God, intellect, and the object understood, and the intelligible species, and his act of understanding are entirely one and the same thing."

5 *Does God know things other than himself?*

Yes. It seems like another obvious answer, but, as one of the objections in this question holds, all other things are outside God, and Augustine once wrote that "God does not behold anything out of himself." (Further, although Thomas does not mention it here, Aristotle, in his *Metaphysics*, spoke of God as "thought thinking thought"—as always involved in contemplating only himself. This certainly suggests an aloofness, and would seem at odds with the idea of God as love, as we'll examine in chapter 20.)

But Scripture has made clear regarding creatures that "all are open and laid bare to the eyes of him with whom we have to do" (Heb. 4:13).

Thomas notes that whatever exists pre-existed in God as its first cause and must lie within his understanding. All things are, therefore, intelligible to him. When God sees himself, "he sees other things not in themselves, but in himself, inasmuch as his essence contains the similitude of things other than himself." (We could say that in seeing himself, God sees all there is to see.) Augustine meant not that God does not see things outside himself, but that "what is outside himself he does not see except in himself, as above explained."

6 *Does God know things other than himself by proper knowledge?*

Yes. This question builds on the previous one and suggests that if God knows things outside himself as he sees them in himself, then perhaps he knows things only in a general, rather than in a specific way. Thomas could hardly disagree more strongly. To know something properly, it is not enough to know it in general; rather, you have to know it as distinct from everything else.

Scripture not only tells us that no creature is hidden from God (Heb. 4:13, as in our last question), but describes God's knowledge as "piercing to the division of soul and spirit, of joints and marrow, and discerning the thoughts and intentions of the heart" (4:12). Indeed, we might recall as well that even before we are formed in the womb, he knows us (Jer. 1:5).

Thomas elaborates that to know a thing in general and not in particular is to have imperfect knowledge. We have seen already that God's knowledge is perfect. Thomas adds that "God could not be said to know himself perfectly unless he knew all the ways in which his own perfection could be shared by others." He knows all things according to all modes of being—with full and proper knowledge of each and every one of us.

7 Is God's knowledge discursive?

No. Perhaps you're asking, "What does *discursive* mean?" Well, I'm going to attempt to explain it to you . . . one step and one word at a time—which, in fact, is what *discursive* means! Our intellects operate on one thing at a time as images are presented to our senses, or as we recall intellectual concepts we have formed in the past. When we use logic or scientific methods to arrive at truth, we must follow careful step-by-step reasoning processes. *Discursive knowledge* is contrasted with *intuition*, in which understanding is obtained in an instant. (Indeed, Thomas writes that the angels, being purely immaterial beings, understand by intuition.) Now, since God is immaterial and purely spiritual, he requires no step-by-step process progressing through bodily organs toward an immaterial intellect. As Augustine wrote in *On the Trinity*, "God does not see all things in the particularity or separately, as if he saw alternately here and there; but he sees all things together at once."

Like the angels, God knows all that he knows all at once. Unlike with the angels, all that he knows is all that there is to know!

8   Is God's knowledge the cause of things?

Yes. I find this question especially interesting in our time. Aristotle wrote in the *Metaphysics* that "the thing known is prior to knowledge and is its measure." In other words, reality comes before our knowledge of it. This is also captured by a once-common aphorism I haven't heard much lately: "Thinking doesn't make it so." We also used to call the denial of this fact *wishful* or even *magical* thinking, yet today, how often we hear people who believe that their thinking can alter realities as fundamental as whether they are male or female!

Now, whereas *our* thoughts in themselves do not cause external realities, indeed, "the knowledge of God is the cause of things." As Augustine wrote, "Not because they are, does God know all creatures spiritual and temporal, but because he knows them, they are." Whereas our thinking doesn't make it so, God's does.

9 Does God have knowledge of things that are not?

Yes. Here is another intellectual doozy. Some argued that even God could not know things that do not exist. God knows true things, and *truth* and *being* are convertible terms, so God would not have knowledge of things that are not.

We see Scripture, however, speaking of God this way: "Who . . . calleth those things that are not as those that are" (Rom. 4:17).* Thomas elaborates that "God knows all things whatsoever that in any way are." Even things that are not absolutely actual reside "in the power either of God himself or of a creature, whether in active power or passive; whether in power of thought or imagination, or of any other manner of meaning whatever." Indeed, whatever can be "made, or thought, or said by the creature, as also whatever he himself can do, all are known to God, although they are not actual." Therefore, he has knowledge, even of things that are not.

Thomas continues, "The present glance of God extends over all time, and to all things which exist in any time, as objects present to him." Even as regards things that have not been and will never be, "he is said to have the knowledge, not of vision, but of simple intelligence."

10 Does God know evil things?

Yes. Some thought he might not. Aristotle wrote in *On the Soul* that "the intellect that is not in potentiality does not know privation. But," as Thomas summarizes the objection, "*evil is*

---

* The RSV-CE renders it "who gives life to the dead and calls into existence the things that do not exist."

the privation of a good, as Augustine says." Therefore, it would seem that God, who is pure act, could not know evil things.

We read in Scripture, to the contrary, that "hell and destruction are before God" (Prov. 15:11), and it doesn't get much more evil than hell.

Thomas elaborates that anyone who knows anything perfectly must also know everything that could be accidental to it, including what could be changed or corrupted in it. Evil is such an accident of corruption. Hence, "God would not know good things perfectly, unless he also knew evil things." What Aristotle meant is that an intellect not in potentiality "does not know privation by privation existing in it." (Evil, as privation, does not exist in and of itself.) The intellect knows evil in relation to the good that should exist in place of it. "God therefore knows evil, not by privation existing in himself, but by the opposite good."

11 *Does God know singular things?*

Yes. Some reasoned to the contrary: Aristotle noted that the human intellect, because it is immaterial, knows *universal* (abstract, generalized) things, rather than *singular* (concrete, individual) things, which are known through sensation via physical, material organs. Since God's intellect is more immaterial than the human intellect (God being purely spirit), it would seem that God does not know singular things.

Scripture tells us, to the contrary, "All the ways of man are open to his eyes" (Prov. 16:2). Thomas tells us God certainly knows singular things, since all perfections possessed by creatures pre-exist in him in a higher way (as we saw in Q. 4., a. 2). We can know singular things, so God must know them, too. Whereas we, as beings composed of body and soul, were made with two faculties—the intellectual, to know universals, and sensation, to know singular things—"God knows both by his simple intellect."

12 Can God know infinite things?

Yes. This is another interesting issue. Some argued that even God could not know infinite things, since the infinite, as Aristotle said in his *Physics*, is that which "to those who measure it leaves always something more to be measured." Augustine added in *The City of God* that "whatever is comprehended by knowledge is bounded by the comprehension of the knower." Since infinite things have no boundary, it would seem that even God's knowledge could not comprehend them.

On the contrary, Augustine qualifies his statement as follows: "Although we cannot number the infinite, nevertheless it can be comprehended by him whose knowledge has no bounds." Recalling that God knows not only actual things, but possible things as well (as we saw in this chapter's ninth question), "as these must be infinite, it must be held that God knows infinite things."

As for Aristotle's observation, it refers to infinite quantity, which implies that the knower knows an order of parts that are known part after part (after part, literally *ad infinitum*!). In this way, an infinity cannot be known, because no matter how many parts are considered, more will always remain.

And here is where things get very interesting: God, Thomas tells us, does not know infinite things as if he had counted them part by part, since he knows everything there is to know "simultaneously, and not successively." So yes, God knows even infinite things.

13 *Does God know future contingent things?*

Yes. Some thought God could not know future contingent or possible things because "whatever God knows is necessary" and not contingent. Therefore, God could not know future things that may or may not happen.

On the contrary, we read of God, in reference to men, referred to as "he who hath made the hearts of every one of them, who understandeth all their works" (Ps. 33 [32]:15).

Thomas notes that the works of men are contingent because they depend upon our free will. Therefore, God knows even future, contingent things. Things that are future and contingent in relation to their causes (like our free will) are future and contingent from our limited perspective, but God infallibly knows them in his eternal now—in Thomas's eloquent words, "because his glance is carried from eternity over all things as they are in their presentiality."

14 *Does God know enunciable things?*

Yes. When I hear the word *enunciation*, my thoughts go back to fourth-grade music class. As we got ready to sing, our teacher, a good Dominican nun named Sr. Wilma Marie, would exhort us to crisply "E-NUN-CI-ATE!" (clearly pronounce) our words. What Thomas has in mind is whether God knows the kinds of things that we express in words in the form of verbal propositions or statements.

Some thought he could not, since our intellects compose and divide and grasp and express things through sequential processes grounded upon images, whereas God's intellect is absolutely simple, without composition.

Scripture tells, us, however, that "the Lord knoweth the thoughts of men" (Ps. 94 [93]: 11). Thomas explains that our intellect gives us the power to formulate thoughts into words and speech, and "since God knows whatever is in his own power or in that of creatures, as said above (a. 9), it follows of necessity that God knows all enumerations that can be formed."

Are you seeing the pattern I'm seeing? It seems that when arguments are made that would limit God's knowledge, the objections tend to treat God as if his knowledge operated like that of human beings, albeit at a higher level. I see this in many arguments of modern atheists as well, who treat God as if he were some ultimate or super-human—vastly more powerful, but still limited by things like time and human processes for reasoning and acquiring knowledge. In a sense, they treat of a God created in our image instead of recalling that we were made in God's image. We are the diverse and imperfect images of the one and perfect original.

To attempt to rein in God with our standards is a perilous venture. It calls to mind a phrase that St. Jerome used in a different context. When some argued that God could not possibly allow souls who were in heaven or hell to leave temporarily, Jerome posed the powerful rhetorical question: "Wouldst thou then lay down the law for God?" Since the divine law of God is the basis of all human and natural law, it's not a good intellectual or "legal" gambit.*

15 Does God's knowledge vary?

No. We saw that God is immutable (Q. 9), and so is his knowledge. We read in Scripture that in God, "there is no change nor shadow of alteration" (James 1:17). Our own

---

* Details on Jerome's question and his opinion on the matter can be found in *ST*, Supplement, Q. 69, a. 3.

knowledge can vary, as when things we thought were true turn out to be false. This is because our reasoning works through step-by-step enunciable processes, as we just discussed. God's knowledge would be variable if it worked like ours, but it doesn't. "Since the knowledge of God is his substance (unlike ours), as is clear from the forgoing (a. 4), just as his substance is altogether immutable, as shown above (Q. 9, a. 1), so his knowledge likewise must be altogether invariable."

16 Does God have speculative knowledge of things?

Yes. Some thought God could not have *speculative* knowledge of the nature of things, because such knowledge is not the cause of things (as *practical* knowledge can be), but we saw that God's knowledge does cause things (a. 8), so God's knowledge could not be speculative. Further, speculative, universal knowledge comes from the intellectual process of abstraction from perceptions produced by the physical senses, but God has no senses.

Thomas rebuts these rather abstract (speculative, perhaps?) ideas by noting that "whatever is the more excellent must be attributed to God" (as the font of all created perfections). Aristotle notes in the *Metaphysics* that speculative knowledge is more excellent than practical knowledge. Therefore, Thomas says, God has speculative knowledge of things.

To make a long explanation short, Thomas addresses different kinds of speculative and practical knowledge and the relationship between the two, the speculative intellect being aimed at "consideration of truth," and "practical intellect is ordered to the end of operation" (which means that it is about applying truths to get particular things done). God has both speculative and practical knowledge to the supreme degree.

As to the objections, God's knowledge does not cause himself (as he is uncaused, self-subsistent being), but he is the cause of other things—of actual things that come to exist in time and of virtual things "that he can make, and which nevertheless are never made." For human beings, speculative knowledge is founded in sensation and perception, but this does not apply to God.

Summa of God's Knowledge

God . . .

1 holds the highest place in the knowledge of things.

2 understands himself.

3 comprehends himself.

4 is one in that his intellect is his substance or essence.

5 knows all things outside himself.

6 knows all things outside himself through proper, particular knowledge.

7 knows all things not discursively, but all at once.

8 causes things through his knowledge.

9 knows even things that are not, but merely exist in potentiality.

10 knows evil things.

11 knows singular, individual things.

12 knows even infinite things.

13 knows even future, contingent or possible things (like human choices and acts).

14 knows enunciable things that humans express in language.

15 is unchangeable in his knowledge, just as he is in his substance.

16 has both speculative and practical knowledge about things.

15

GOD'S
IDEAS

He has ideas of all things known to him.

ST, I, Q. 15, a. 3

Have you ever told someone, "That's a good idea"? What exactly *is* an idea, and does *God* have ideas? St. Thomas tells us that after considering God's knowledge, we should consider ideas.

1 Are there ideas?

Yes. Thomas explains that the Greek word *idea* is translated into Latin as *forma* (form). This means that by ideas, we understand the forms of things, as existing separate from the things themselves (as when we understand the idea of *dog*, or *human*, in general, beyond particular individuals like, let's say, Spot or Sally).

Some argued that ideas could not really exist. Dionysius said in *The Divine Names* that God does not know things by ideas, and yet ideas are nothing else than that by which things are known, so ideas cannot exist. Further, we saw that God sees all things in himself (Q. 14, a. 5), and not through ideas, so other things must not exist as ideas, either.

Thomas counters with the words of St. Augustine: "Such is the power in ideas, that no one can be wise unless they are understood."

Thomas, having connected ideas with the grasp of things' forms, then elaborates that such forms existing apart from things can be for one of two ends:

A "to be the *type* of that which it is called the form, or"

B "to be the *principle of the knowledge* of that thing, inasmuch as the forms of things knowable are said to be in him who knows them."

In either case, these *forms* suppose *ideas*. Let's see how. To begin, for anything that does not come about purely by chance or random events, "the form must be the end of any generation whatever." (Recall that a formal cause is what makes something "into that which" it is.) But no causal agent acts on account of its form unless there is a likeness of the form within the agent. This can happen in two ways:

A In some agents, the form of the thing to be made pre-exists in its maker "according to its natural being," like when humans beget humans or fire generates fire.

■ In other agents, "the form of the thing to be made pre-exists according to the intelligible being, as in those that act by the intellect." Take for example the case of a house that pre-exists in the mind of its builder. The builder strives to build a house like the form (idea or concept) conceived in his mind.

Well, since the universe did not come about by chance but was made by God acting through his intellect (as Thomas tells us he'll flesh out in I, Q. 46, a. 1 on whether the universe and creatures always existed), "there must exist in the divine mind a form to the likeness of which the world was made. And in this the notion of an idea consists."

As to Dionysius's statement, Thomas notes that Plato promulgated the opinion that ideas actually exist in themselves, and not in the intellect, which Aristotle rightly rejected. God does understand by an idea, but not by an idea that lies outside himself. Whereas God knows himself by his own essence, his essence is the operating principle in every created thing outside himself. "It has therefore the nature of an idea with respect to other things; though not with respect to himself."

2 Are there many ideas?

Yes. It seemed to some that there could be only one idea. What gave them that idea? Well, one argument held that an idea in God is his essence, but God's essence, as we've seen (Q. 11), is *one*.

Thomas starts by citing Augustine, who said (to paraphrase) that ideas are principal forms, or permanent and unchanging things that in themselves are not formed. They are eternal and always exist in the same way because they are contained in God's divine intelligence. Still, although the ideas themselves have no beginning or end, it is through ideas that every thing is formed that can come to be, decay, and all the rest.

Thomas elaborates that there then must be many ideas, though some are more fundamental than others. He notes that for every effect, the ultimate end or sake for which it exists is "the proper intention of the principal agent, as the order of an army [is the proper intention] of the general." As Aristotle points out, "The highest of all existing things is the good of the order of the universe."

So the order of the universe is intended by God like the order of the army by its general. It is not an accidental result of a series of subsequent causal agents, as was believed by those who argued that God created only the first, highest creature, which then created the second, and so on, until we had the multitude of beings that fill the universe. In that erroneous view, God would have only that one idea of the first created thing. Thomas counters that God must have the idea of the order of the universe, and there can't be an idea of the whole unless there are also particular ideas of the parts out of which a whole can be made—a builder can't form his idea of a house unless he has ideas regarding its parts. "So then it must needs be that in the divine mind there are proper ideas of all things."

This in no way contradicts the simplicity of God's mind. He knows things not through many images, but because he perfectly knows his own essence, from which all things flow.

As for the objection we started with, God's essence is not an idea. There are many ideas because "many types are understood through the selfsame essence."

3 Are there ideas of all things God knows?

Yes, though there are some interesting philosophical arguments that might indicate otherwise. Consider, for example, that we saw in Q. 15, a. 9 that God knows even of things that do not exist, will not exist, and never did. Dionysius wrote that "acts of the divine will are the effective and determining types of all things." God, then, could not have ideas of things that he has not caused and determined. Further, consider that God knows primary matter, which has no form, and therefore can be no idea.

These are interesting conundrums, perhaps, but Thomas, as you might expect by now, has some pretty good ideas for solving them. He reminds us that ideas are types that exist in the divine mind, and God has the types of all things he knows, and therefore he has the ideas of all things he knows.

Thomas borrows from Plato, who wrote that ideas are principles of the knowledge of things and of their generation (how they are made), and "an idea has this twofold office, as it exists in the mind of God." Let's peek in the door of this twofold office of ideas:

A As regarding the principle of *making things*, an idea is called an *exemplar* and exists as a component of *practical* knowledge.

B But so far as an idea is a principle of *knowledge*, it is called a *type* (we sometimes use the word *archetype*) and belongs to *speculative* knowledge.

So an idea as an *exemplar* relates to anything God has made in any period of time (creatable things that actually do, will, or did exist), and an idea as a *type* relates to all things God knows, even if they never come to be in time (purely knowable things), "and to all things that he knows according to their proper type, insofar as he knows them speculatively" as they are in themselves.

Summa of God's Ideas

Ideas (or concepts) . . .

1 are the means by which the intellect grasps the essence of things, by mentally abstracting the form of the thing from the matter in which it is clothed, as we understand the *universal* idea of *humanity* that exists in real, physical, individual people. God has ideas, but they do not come from outside himself. He knows himself and all things by knowing his own essence, from which all things flow.

2 are many, even in the mind of God, not in that he requires a plurality of ideas, as we do, but many ideas exist in the mind of God, even in his utter simplicity, because he perfectly knows his essence, from which all things flow.

3 are in the mind of God for all things, whether the things actually exist (in which case he knows them as practical *exemplars*) or do not exist, have not existed, and will never exist (in which case he knows them as speculative *types*).

16

GOD IS
TRUTH

Whence it follows that not only is
truth in him, but that he is truth itself,
and the sovereign and first truth.

ST, I, Q. 16, a. 5

When Pontius Pilate asked Jesus, "What is truth?" (John 8:37), he did not wait for an answer. But if we are patient, we will soon receive eight answers from St. Thomas Aquinas on the true nature of truth—and one of those answers will reveal that Pontius Pilate was staring truth right in the face at the time of his question. Thomas begins by telling us, tersely enough, that since knowledge is about things that are true, having considered knowledge it is time to consider *truth*.

1   *Does truth exist only in the intellect?*

Not *only*, but *primarily*. Today, some people embrace such a relativistic view of truth that they speak of "your truth" and "my truth," or say "that is true for you, and this is true for me." Not only in the sense that perhaps you believe that spicy foods are delicious and I don't, but in the sense that "truth" in general is whatever you or I decide it is for us— that thinking really does make things so, external reality be damned. According to such radical relativism, truth is whatever anybody believes (or wants to believe) it is, and it therefore does reside only in the intellect (regardless of how distorted or contorted someone's intellect may be). We used to classify extreme relativistic beliefs as psychosis—a loss of mental contact with external reality.

When Thomas addressed the issue in the thirteenth century, the objections he presented held the opposite extreme opinion in that truth resided not in our intellect but in things themselves. Augustine, for example, declared, "That is true which is." Aristotle also wrote, "That on account of which a thing is so, is itself more so. But whether our thoughts or words are true or false derives from the fact that a thing is or is not what we think or say it is. Therefore, truth resides rather in things than in the intellect."

Thomas was quite aware, however, that Aristotle also made clear that "the true and the false reside not in things, but in the intellect." Thomas's fine-tuned analysis nicely clears things up (and rings true).

He begins with a comparison of the *good* and the *true*. Our *appetites* reach out toward the *good*, whereas our intellect tends toward the *true*. As the good is to appetite, truth is to the intellect.

There is a crucial difference between appetite and intellect: the appetite tends to the thing *desired*, whereas the knowledge of the intellect "is according as the thing *known* is in the knower." So the term or end of *appetite* is the *object desired*, whereas the term or end of the *intellect*—namely, what's true—is *in the intellect itself.*

Still, the true resides in the intellect only when it is "conformed to" or corresponds to the object the intellect understands, so "the aspect of the true must needs pass from the intellect to the object understood, so that also the thing understood is said to be true insofar that it has some relation to the intellect." (So truth certainly does involve both the intellect *and* the object of external reality.)

As for *the primacy of the intellect* regarding truth, we judge things according to their essences rather than their mere accidents. Whatever is said to be true absolutely is related to the intellect "from which it depends," as *artificial* or *man-made things* are called true as they are related to our intellect. An architect will call a house true when it bears a likeness to what he had in his mind when he designed it. Words are called true when they are signs of truth in the intellect. In this sense, not only artificial but *natural* things are rightly called true "insofar as they express the likeness of the species that are in the divine mind." Indeed, Thomas tells us that even a stone is called true when it possesses the true nature of a stone as it pre-existed in God's mind.

So truth is *primarily* of the intellect—because even external, objective, artificial, and natural things obtain their own essence from an intellect, human or divine—but truth does reside *secondarily* in things—"as they are related to the intellect as their principle."

Because the nature of truth entails an intertwining of intellect and things, Thomas notes that there are several definitions of truth. He lays out some of them for us:

- Per Augustine: "Truth is that whereby is made manifest that which is."

- Per Hilary of Poitiers: "Truth makes being clear and evident."

- Per Anselm of Canterbury: "Truth is rightness, perceptible by the mind alone."

- Per Avicenna (Persian philosopher Ibn-Sina): "The truth of each thing is a property of the essence which is immutably attached to it."

- Per Thomas himself: "Truth is the equation of thought and thing."

So, regarding particular external realities, "your truth" and "my truth" will both be simply "the truth" only when our thoughts accurately correspond to things as they are in themselves.

Perhaps one area where this idea needs to be reinforced today is in the realm of the science of biology. For example, regardless of how two people might "identify" themselves, it is true that only an individual with an XY pair of chromosomes (a male) and an individual with an XX pair of chromosomes (a female) can reproduce another human being. Thinking otherwise does not make it so. External reality has an important role to play.

2 Are truth and being convertible (interchangeable) terms?

Yes. Although we saw in our first question of this chapter that the true, strictly speaking, is in the intellect, and the good in things, Thomas sides with Aristotle, who says "that there is the same disposition of things in being and truth." What is good is desirable, and what is true is knowable. This is why Aristotle wrote that "'the soul is in some manner all things,' through the sense and the intellect. And therefore, as good is convertible with being, so is the true. But as good adds to the notion of desirable, so the true adds relation to the intellect."

As we saw when examining how *good* and *being* are convertible terms, in that they differ not in reality but in idea (Q. 6, a. 1), a similar situation applies to *true* and *being*. Again, we saw in our first question of this chapter that truth resides in the *intellect* primarily and in *things* secondarily. Therefore, "truth and being differ in idea" but are, in reality, convertible terms.

3 Does the good come before the true?

No. To be more precise, Thomas phrases this question, "Whether the Good is Logically Prior to the True?" One simple argument to the contrary notes that good is in things and truth in the intellect composing and dividing (as we saw in our second question). "But that which is in things is prior to that which is in the intellect. Therefore the good is logically prior to the true."

"Not so fast!" says Thomas. To say something is logically prior is to say it is prior in terms of the intellect. Note that the first thing the intellect apprehends is "being itself"; next, it "apprehends that it understands being"; and finally, "it apprehends that it desires being." Therefore, in the human intellect, the logical order of apprehension is as follows: first *being*, then *truth*, and finally *good*.

I want to point out an interesting moral lesson captured within a third objection and Thomas's reply. The objection notes that Aristotle defines truth as a specific kind of virtue, but virtue is a kind of subset of the good, since Augustine said virtue is a "good quality of the mind." Hence, it would seem that the good is prior to the true.

The point worth noting here appears in Thomas's reply. Aristotle referred not to truth in general, but to "a certain kind of truth according to which man shows himself in deed and word as he really is." Aristotle was referring to a particular virtue, which we might think of as "honesty," that serves the cardinal virtue of *justice*. Justice requires that we give one another our rightful due, and we owe it to each other to speak truthfully. And as God told us in the eighth commandment, "You shall not bear false witness against your neighbor" (Exod. 20:16). Indeed, later in the *Summa* (II-II, Q. 109, "Of Truth"), Thomas examines truth in the sense of this virtue in four insightful articles.

4 Is God truth?

Yes. Here we will see what it means to say that when Pilate asked Jesus, "What is truth?", he was staring truth in the face.

Some thought God could not *be* truth, for various reasons. For example, we saw that truth resides in the "composing and dividing" reasoning process of the intellect, but there is no composition and division in God, who knows everything simultaneously. Therefore, some thought, we cannot say God is truth.

Thomas responds in the words that Jesus spoke not to Pilate, but previously to his disciples: "I am the way, and the truth, and the life" (John 14:7). Later in the *Summa*, Thomas addresses in depth how Jesus is God—in his discussions of the Trinity in I, Qs. 27-43 and of Jesus Christ in particular in III, Qs. 1-59), but for now, Thomas, in his "I answer that" section, gives a fascinating explanation of God as truth that warrants repeating in full:

> As said above (A. 1), truth is found in the intellect according as it apprehends a thing as it is; and in things according as they have being conformable to an intellect. This is to the greatest degree found in God. For his being is not only conformed to his intellect, but is the very act of his intellect, and his act of understanding is the measure and cause of every other being and of every other intellect, and he himself is his own existence and act of understanding. Whence it follows not only that truth is in him, but that he is truth itself, and the sovereign and first truth.

Our thinking does not make things so, but *God's thought does*.

As for the objection: truth to human beings is a matter of composing and dividing with our limited intellectual powers, but God knows the complexity of all things with "his simple act of intelligence, and thus there is truth in his intellect."

5 Is there only one truth?

No. Recalling that truth is primarily in the intellect and secondarily in things, as those things are related to the divine intellect there are as many truths as there are created intellects (as within all human beings and angels). Further, there are many truths in these many created intellects, and even within the same individual intellect, according to the number of things the owner of that intellect knows.

Still, "if we speak of truth as it is in things, then all things are true by one primary truth." Although there are many essences and forms of things, "the truth of the divine intellect is one, in conformity to which all things are said to be true."

6 Is created truth eternal?

No. One objection brings in mathematical concepts and cites Augustine's observation that "nothing is more eternal than the nature of a circle, and that two added to three make five." But the truth of a circle and of addition are created truths, which implies that created truths are also eternal.

But nothing created is in itself eternal. As we saw in chapter 10, God alone is eternal. Thomas notes further that truth is eternal only in God. Humans can grasp eternal truths, but these truths are true in themselves because God eternally knows them to be true. Even things like the nature of a circle and the fact that two plus three equals five are not merely created things, but "have eternity in the mind of God."

7 Is truth unchangeable?

No—or at least not in created intellects, but only in the

divine intellect. We read in Scripture that "truths are decayed from the children of men" (Ps. 12 [11]:2).

Recalling that truth resides primarily in the intellect and is the conformity between the thing (i.e., external reality) and the intellect, the conformity may vary or change in two ways:

A as regards the *intellect*, when there is a change of opinion about something that has not in itself changed, or

B as regards the *thing*, when the thing itself has changed, but not the opinion.

In either case, the intellect can move from truth to falsity.

Allow me to flesh this out with a simple example. As regarding the first way, let's say I desire to eat what I consider a perfectly good apple, which it is, but someone I assume to be trustworthy falsely warns me that it has been poisoned. (After all, recall that truths do decay in the minds of men, and people do lie to their neighbors.) In this case, the truth that was in my intellect regarding that apple has changed to a false opinion, and it was not the apple's fault, for the apple did not change. (Come to think of it, this scenario was played out in the reverse with Eve and the serpent in the garden of Eden!)

As for the second way, let's say the apple truly has been poisoned. and I don't know it (or perhaps it has been swapped out with one from the tree of knowledge!). If I still think the apple good, my opinion, remaining the same, has changed from true to false, because the thing itself has changed.

These distinctions apply only to created intellects, however. As Thomas makes clear, if there is an intellect that simply cannot be fooled, that has no changes in opinion whatsoever, because "the knowledge of which nothing can escape," then "in this is immutable truth." Therefore, whereas truth is surely changeable in our intellects, as it may move from truth to falsity, truth in God's divine intellect is as utterly unchangeable as he is.

Summa of God and Truth

Truth . . .

1 is the equation of thought and thing, residing primarily in the intellect and secondarily in things.

2 resides in the mind of man through his reasoning processes, but simply and completely in the mind of God.

3 is a convertible or interchangeable term with *being* in reality, but these do differ in idea, truth residing primarily in the intellect and being residing primarily in things.

4 is logically prior to the good within the intellect.

5 is God—or more properly arranged, God *is* truth.

6 is many within the minds of created intellectual beings, but one according to the primary truth of the divine intellect.

7 is eternal as it exists in the mind of God.

8 can change within the minds of creatures, but is immutable within the mind of God.

17

GOD AND
FALSITY

In things that depend on God,
falseness cannot be found.

ST, I, Q. 17, a. 1

After considering truth, St. Thomas states merely, "We next consider falsity" and lays out four questions he will address before he dives right in.

1 *Does falsity exist in things?*

Yes, but only in a secondary, accidental sense. It may appear reasonable to argue that falsity exists not in *things*, but in the *intellect*, as does truth. Further, the word *false* is derived from the Latin word *fallere*, which means to deceive (as we see in English words like *fallacy* and *fallacious*). Things do not deceive, but merely show what they are. Moreover, truth is a matter of conformity to the divine intellect, as we saw in our last chapter, yet everything that exists imitates God. Therefore, no existing thing is false.

Thomas cites Augustine as he begins his nuanced rebuttal: "Every body is a true body and false unity; for it imitates unity without being unity." In other words, everything does imitate God in his divine unity, but falls short of true, complete unity. *In that sense*, we can say that falsity exists in things.

Thomas continues that true and false are opposites, and opposites are opposed in their relation to the same thing. *Since truth is primarily in the intellect, so is falsity.* So, *in things*, neither truth nor falsity exists, "except in relation to the intellect."

In an analysis similar to what we saw in the first question of our last chapter on how truth resides primarily in the intellect, Thomas compares truth and falsity in relation to artificial (man-made) and natural (God-created) things. Artificial things can be called false in and of themselves "when they fall short of the form of the art," as when a craftsman produces a faulty work that falls short of what he intended. (For example, we might call a table that collapses as soon as it is set on its legs a false table—"You call *that* a table?")

As for natural things that depend on God, there is no falseness to be found in how they compare to the divine intellect. (God makes no mistakes!) Yet we may see an exception of sorts in the case of voluntary agents (like us, beings who have free will). We can choose to withdraw ourselves from God's intention, and this is what we call *sin*. Therefore, sins are untruths or falsities. Indeed, we see this idea expressed in Scripture: "Why do you love vanity and seek after lying?" (Ps. 4:3), and "He that doth truth, cometh to the light" (John 3:21).

False opinions about things can arise in us because of the way our cognitive processes depend on information that our senses bring us. We can and do make mistakes in interpreting things we sense. Augustine says, "We call those things false that appear to the apprehension like true." Aristotle chimes in that "things are called false that are naturally apt to appear such as they are not, or what they are not." Thomas gives one example of tin being called "false gold," because it can look enough like gold that some people may confuse them. In our day, we speak of "fool's gold" (shiny pyrite mineral clusters) in a similar way.

We might include as well the whole realm of "optical illusions," where we are led to misinterpret what we see, and even everyday phenomena (like when my wife calls out to me to look into the backyard to help her determine if what she sees lying on the ground way back there is a leaf or some small animal). Such falsity lies not primarily within the things themselves, since tin, gold, leaves, and small animals, and even optical illusions, truly are what they are in themselves. As Thomas says, "Things do not deceive us by their own nature, but by accident." Ultimately, we deceive ourselves!

2   Is falsity in our senses?

No. Our senses accurately report the forms of the things they detect, barring a defect in a sense organ, as when something sweet seems bitter to a sick person with a diseased tongue. If we are deceived by the information we obtain from our senses, it derives from a false judgment in the intellect.

An example I recall hearing decades ago about the supposed unreliability of the senses: when seen under water, a straight stick looks as though it is bent, hence, our senses (in this case, our "lying eyes"!) have deceived us. Thomas says that in such cases "we are deceived by sense about the object [the stick in our example], but not about the fact of sensation." In this case, the "fact of sensation" has reflected the fact that water refracts (bends) light. Our senses have revealed the truth of this refraction to us. If we falsely believe that the straight stick is bent, we must blame our intellect for its ignorance of the fact of refraction, and not our "truthful eyes."

This fact is of crucial importance, by the way, to the entire Aristotelian–Thomistic understanding of human cognition. Ideas in our intellect are not in themselves *what* we think about, but *that by which* we think about things. Our ideas are formed based on impressions we receive from our sense. Our senses can be trusted to reflect external realities and to lead us to truth and not falsity, if we interpret sense-knowledge carefully with our intellectual powers.

3 Is falsity in our intellect?

Yes. I imagine you've deduced by now that falsity does reside primarily in our minds. Aristotle deduced as much over twenty-three centuries ago! Thomas points out that Aristotle wrote that "where there is composition of objects understood, there is truth and falsehood." As we saw earlier (Q. 16, a. 2), it is precisely the intellect that "composes and divides." Truth and falsehood do exist in the intellect.

Our senses relay reliable information (raw data, we might say) about the outside world, and it is up to our intellect to cast judgments about that information. Now, just as "sense is directly informed by the likeness of its proper object, so is the intellect by the likeness of the essence of a thing." So, in the simple act of apprehension of essence, the intellect is not deceived. The possibility of error and belief in a falsehood arises in the judgments of the intellect. "But in affirming and denying, the intellect may be deceived, by attributing to the thing of which it understands the essence, something which is not consequent upon it, or opposed to it."

So our senses and intellects were created with the capacity to grasp the truths of reality. False opinions (intellectual mistakes or errors) are not due to the substance of our powers and sensation. Those are not substantially flawed. Rather, false opinions arise from an accidental misuse or misapplication of our intellectual powers—for example, when we jump to false conclusions about a given situation because we have not gathered and considered all of the relevant facts.

As for God, there is no falsity whatever in God's divine intellect. He has no need to "compose and divide" as we do, for, as we have seen, God is all-knowing (Q. 14) and, indeed, is truth itself (Q. 16)!

4 Are true and false contraries?

Yes, and this may seem a fine point, but it's worth noting. Falsity is not merely a *negation*, a lack of truth or the denial of a truth, but the *assertion* of something contrary to proof in its place. Thomas paraphrases Aristotle, who noted that "falsity asserts something, for a thing is false . . . inasmuch as something is said or seems to be something that is not, or not to be what it really is." As falsity related to our conceptions of God, as an example of asserting something to be what it is not, we might think of those who believe that idols are gods. For an example of asserting something not to be what it really is, we might think of those who assert that God is merely a figment of man's imagination: "The fool says in his heart, 'There is no God'" (Ps. 14 [13]:1).

Thomas elaborates that truth implies "an adequate apprehension of a thing, so falsity implies the contrary. It is clear that true and false are contraries." The same statement cannot be both true and false in the same sense, at the same time. (Just try answering both true and false on a true-or-false test at school, or telling your professor that the statements might be true for him, but not for you, and, truly, you will not be pleased with your score!)

Summa of God and Falsity

Falsity . . .

1 exists not in things, except in relation to the imperfect, created intellect.

2 exists not in the senses or intellectual apprehensions themselves, but in the judgments

3 the intellect casts upon them.

4 resides in the intellect as it composes and divides (judges, reasons), and resides not at all in the divine intellect, which does not compose and divide, being all-knowing and, indeed, truth itself.

5 is the contrary of truth, asserting that something to be that is not, or asserting something is not that really is.

PART V

HOW DOES GOD
LIVE
(AND LOVE)?

The love of God infuses and creates goodness.

ST, I, Q. 20, a. 2

18

GOD'S
LIFE

Life is in the highest degree properly in God.

ST, I, Q. 18, a. 3

St. Thomas tells us that since understanding belongs to living beings, after having considered the divine knowledge and intellect, we will turn to the divine life.

1   *Do all natural things possess life?*

No (as I'm pretty sure you are aware already!). Still, some people well versed in Aristotle know that he said, "Movement is like a kind of life possessed by things existing in nature." Further, though elements are among the least perfect natural bodies, we even speak of "living waters." Therefore, in a sense, all natural things possess life.

Thomas starts his response with a line from Dionysius: "The last echo of life is heard in plants." In other words, plants possess life in its lowest degree. He then notes that we can gauge what things can be considered to possess life by comparing them to things that possess life without question, and here he turns to animals. An animal is said to be living when it can move itself. When it can no longer do so, but can only be moved by another power, the animal's life is gone, and the animal is dead. (What was once a living animal is now a carcass.)

So, not merely things that move, but things that *move themselves* are living things.

Aristotle was speaking in terms of similitude: any kind of movement in a natural thing is merely similar in some ways to the movement of living things. In an analogy that would not have been used in Aristotle's day (or even in Thomas's), we might note how swiftly an automobile or an airplane moves, but we know that neither is a living thing. The same applies to simple elements like "living waters." We call waters living that continually flow and standing waters "dead" (as in the Dead Sea), but all waters consist in fact of only unliving elements (hydrogen and oxygen) without the life-giving form we call a soul. Bodies of water may house elaborate ecosystems bristling with living things, but the water itself is not alive. It cannot grow, take in nourishment, and reproduce like even the tiniest of micro-organisms that call it home.

Although plants might not seem to qualify as self-moving,

they do possess "vital movement" as they gather and move nutrients throughout their tissues in the processes of nutrition, growth, and reproduction. (Indeed, Aristotle and Thomas write elsewhere how roots are to plants as mouths are to animals.) Hence, plants are indeed the "last echo of life," but living things they are.

2 Is life an operation?

No. Some thought it might be. For example, Aristotle distinguished four kinds of life: "Nourishment, sensation, local movement, and understanding. It would appear therefore, that these actions or operations are what define life."

Thomas knew well, however, that Aristotle also wrote, "In living things to live is to be." When our intellect grasps the essence of anything, it does so by abstracting the form from the sensations and perception provided by our senses. "Hence from external appearances we come to the knowledge of the essence of things." When we observe self-movement in some kind in a thing and thus call it living, we signify not the act of self-movement itself, but "a substance to which self-movement and the application of itself to any kind of operation, belong naturally."

To live is to live according to a thing's nature. Living is not something accidental to self-movement, but is "an essential predicate." That a particular living creature moves itself or carries out other operations (such as intellectual processes of understanding and reasoning) follows from is substance. Life is the *source* and *principal* of self-movement primarily, and the *operation* of self-movement secondarily.

3 Is it proper to attribute life to God?

Yes. Some thought it did not make sense to attribute life to God. We saw that self-movement is essential to life, but God does not move (pass from one potential place or state into another), since he is pure act. Further, Aristotle states that "the soul is the cause and principle of the living body." (Note that when we distinguish between *animate* "living" and *inanimate* "nonliving" objects, the distinction is based upon whether or not the being possess an *anima*, the Latin word for "soul.") The principal operation of any soul is to give life. Well, some argued that God has no principle, and therefore we should not say he possesses life!

To the contrary, we read in Scripture, "My heart and my flesh rejoiced in the living God" (Ps. 83:3). God is alive, all right. Indeed, "life is in the highest degree in God."

Thomas proceeds through an examination of some of the distinguishing features of the hierarchy of living things. Let's lay this out in brief:

A The *vegetative soul* is the principle of life in the plant world, and its primary "powers" or operations of self-movement are nutrition, growth, and reproduction.

B The *sensitive soul* is the principle of life in the animal world. Although it possesses the vegetive powers, it also possesses powers of sensing external things, having appetites or desires for certain external things, and powers of local movement to move toward desirable things and to avoid undesirable things. (These powers vary within the animal kingdom, with shelled animals like clams having the least power of local self-movement.)

C The *intellectual soul* is unique on earth to human beings, and although it also possesses vegetative and sensitive powers, it can understand abstract principles and essences, allowing for concept formation and rational thought processes. Further, although it is fed information from the bodily senses, the intellect itself is *immaterial* and *immortal*. (Hence, as Thomas details in the Supplement of the *Summa*, after our bodily death, our souls will live on in heaven, hell, or purgatory until God reunites them with our bodies after Christ's second coming.) Note the qualifier that it is unique "on earth" to human beings. Angels, too, have intellectual souls, yet they are pure spirit, having no ties to a physical body. Their knowledge comes not through physical senses, but through instant intuitions from God or higher angels.

So where does God fit in to the hierarchy of life? We've seen often enough that God is pure spirit and the divine intellect is absolutely infinite. Well, the intellects even of man and the angels at the pinnacle of life are moved by things outside them. Therefore, only a being whose act of understanding is its nature, being moved by nothing outside itself, possesses life in the highest possible degree. This being is God alone, who is sometimes called the *Unmoved Mover*.

As for the idea that God has no principle of life, Thomas reminds us that God is his own existence and understanding, and is therefore his own life, requiring no other principle.

4 *Whether all things are life in God?*

Yes, and I've used Thomas's own wording for this particular question, since it's not the kind of question you hear every day. I'll begin with one objection based on a verse from Scripture we've cited a time or two before: "In him we live, and move, and be" (Acts 17:28). The objection continues that "not all things in God are movement. Therefore, not all things are life in him."

Thomas responds, to the contrary, with this verse: "What was made, in him was life" (John 1:3, 4). He continues that all things were made except for God. Hence, all things are indeed life in God.

We must be careful not to apply the limitations of created beings to God. We saw in the question above that in God, to live is to understand. Further, "in God intellect, the thing understood, and the act of understanding, are one and the same. Hence whatever is in God as understood is the very living or life of God. Now, wherefore, since all things that have been made by God are in him as things understood, it follows that all things in him are the divine life itself." All things God knows are in God's life, and God knows all things. (God's life is truly rich and full beyond reckoning!)

As for the scriptural declaration that we live, and move, and be in him, we must note a twofold meaning. First, our living, moving, and being are *caused* by God. But in a second sense, things are said to be in God as him who *knows* them, and in this sense, all things are in God "through their proper ideas, which in God are not distinct from the divine essence." Therefore, all things are in God as they are in the divine essence. Recall that the divine essence is *life* and not merely *movement*. Hence, it follows that things exist in God not as movement, but as life.

Summa of God's Life

Life . . .

1 is found only in self-moving beings with souls (*animate* beings).

2 is a matter of a thing's essence, rather than merely its operations or acts.

God . . .

3 possesses life in the highest degree, perfect and eternal.

4 is life as he is knowledge in his divine simplicity. All things in God's knowledge are in God's life, so "all things are life in God."

19

GOD'S
WILL

We must hold that the will of God is the cause of
things; and that he acts by the will, and not, as some
have supposed, by a necessity of his nature.

ST, I, Q. 19, a. 4

After examining things pertaining to the divine knowledge,
St. Thomas says we'll consider what belongs to the divine
will. And surely, we know Thomas well enough by now
that if God has *a will*, Thomas will find *a way* to explain it to
us! In fact, Thomas will provide a full dozen questions and
answers, and I will try to keep them short and sweet.

1 Is there will in God?

Yes, but there were some interesting reasons to suspect that he might not possess a will. After all, the will moves us toward objects we desire as good ends or goals, and God certainly has no ends outside himself. Further, will has been called an intellectual appetite that directs us to things we do not possess. This implies imperfection, and we've seen that God is perfect. Finally, Aristotle tells us the will moves and is moved, but, as we've seen, God is the Unmoved Mover.

Thomas begins his reply with Scripture: "That you may prove what is the will of God" (Rom. 12:2). He then elaborates that there is will in God, just as there is intellect, since the will flows from or follows upon the intellect. All things have an appetite toward or aptitude for what is good for them. If this aptitude to the good is done without intellectual knowledge (as in animals relying upon instinct), it is called *natural appetite*. When intellectual creatures apprehend the forms of things that are good for them, they seek to possess and rest in them, and this intellectual appetite we call the *will*. In every intellectual being there is will, just as in every sensible being (animals with sensitive souls) there is animal appetite. Therefore, there must be will in God, since he possesses intellect. Indeed, "as his intellect is his own existence, so is his will."

As for our objections, first off, although God has no ends outside himself, "he himself is the end with respect to all things made by him. And this by his essence, for by his essence he is good (Q. 6, a. 3): for the end has the aspect of good." (The objection, it seems, is another case of attempting to limit God by applying imperfect characteristics of creatures to their perfect Creator.)

The same scenario holds in the second objection. Whereas the will within a creature must move it toward good outside itself, God already possesses all good, so his will is not distinct from his essence.

Finally, when the object of the will is some good outside itself, then the will must indeed be moved. Yet the object of God's divine will is his divine goodness, which is also his essence. Therefore, God is not moved by anything outside himself, but by himself alone. When Plato (Aristotle's teacher) said the first mover moves itself, he meant it "in the same sense as understanding and willing are said to be movement." God wills and moves himself in these ways.

2 Does God will things apart from himself?

Yes. Though God needs no external things and has no ends outside himself, it is in the nature of even the natural will not only to seek and possess its own good, but to share good with others. Every active agent is perfect to the extent that it produces its like. (I'm reminded here of Thomas's statement on the nature of the virtue of science or knowledge that "a characteristic of one possessing science is his ability to teach.") It is in the nature of the will to seek to pass on to others, as far as possible, the good that it possesses. Even more does this apply to the divine will, since every perfection comes from some kind of likeness to God.

God wills both himself and created things to be, with himself as the end, and creatures as aimed to that end, "since it befits the divine goodness that other things should be partakers therein." God's will reaches out even to you and me. As St. Paul tells us, "This is the will of God, your sanctification" (1 Thess. 4:3).

3 Does God will whatever he wills necessarily?

Yes and no. Let's set that stage with a look at the human will. Later in the *Summa*, when focusing on the human will, we find that Augustine says, "All desire happiness with one will," and Thomas agrees, saying, "The will desires something of necessity." This does not mean, as some modern deterministic psychologists and philosophers hold, that we have no free will—that our acts are determined for us and are not our responsibility. Indeed, Thomas retorts to deniers of free will that "man has free will; otherwise counsels, exhortations, commands, prohibitions, rewards, and punishments would be in vain" (*ST*, I, Q. 83, a. 1).

If the will is necessitated to desire the good, how can we have free will? Thomas says the proper act of free will is choice. We have *freedom of exercise* to choose whether to employ our wills one way or another in a given situation. (Surely procrastinators can attest to this!) We have *freedom of specification* to select one thing or course of action while rejecting others. Our free choice is not in regard to the end or goal: we always want happiness. What we choose is the means to that end. It is through our ability to choose or not to choose among different means that we exercise free will and become active, nondetermined agents—masters of our own actions and worthy of praise or blame.*

Now, with a little better understanding of *human* will, free will, and necessity under our belts, let's see what Thomas has to say about *God's* will.

---

* For a look at some neuroscientists and social psychologists who claim, on the basis of simple and flawed experiments, that they have disproved the existence of free will, I recommend Alfred R. Mele, *Free: Why Science Hasn't Disproved Free Will* (New York: Oxford University Press, 2014).

He begins with another verse from Paul, regarding God "who worketh all things according to the counsel of his will" (Eph. 1:11). Thomas says whatever we work out "according to the counsel" of our will, we will not *necessarily*, but after a process of weighing and selecting a course of action. God, therefore, does not will necessarily according to his will, either.

We must make a crucial distinction between two ways in which a thing can be said to be necessary: either *absolutely* or *by supposition*. It is absolutely necessary, for example, that man is an animal or that a number is either odd or even, but it is not necessary that Socrates sits. That is, it is not necessary *absolutely* that Socrates sits (since he may well decide to stand up, lie down, go for a walk, etc.), but it may be necessary *by supposition* as long as Socrates is, in fact, sitting.

Now, there is a sense in which God wills of absolute necessity in that "he wills his own goodness necessarily, even as we will our own happiness." But God wills creatures apart from himself "in so far as they are ordered to his own goodness as their end." He leaves it up to us to choose our means toward that end, as when we choose to travel to some city as our end, we can choose whether we will get there by ship or horseback or foot.

To sum things up, since God is perfect and can exist without any other things, in that they do not add to his perfection, it is not absolutely necessary that he will things apart from himself. Still, his will regarding other things can be considered necessary in that secondary sense, by supposition, for supposing that God wills something, he cannot unwill it, because his will is unchangeable.

4 Does God's will cause things?

Yes, though some have believed that God must act as he acts by a necessity of his *nature* rather than his *will*. One argument held that what is first in any order is first by its essence or nature, so that for burning things, for example, what comes first is fire by its essence. Since God is the first agent of all things, he acts by his essence—that is, his nature—and not by will. Therefore, God's will is not the cause of things.

Thomas begins his response with this piece of inspired wisdom: "How could anything endure, if thou wouldst not?" (Wis. 11:26).* Thomas then tells us that God's will is indeed the cause of things, and that he acts by the will, and not by a necessity of his nature. Further, he says this can be shown in three ways:

A   Aristotle has shown that both intellectual and natural (non-intellectual) agents act for ends, but natural agents must have their ends determined for them by some higher intellect, as in the example Thomas gave of the archer who chooses the arrow's target. So an intellectual and voluntary agent must precede a natural agent that acts according to its nature. Since

---

* Note that Thomas says that as the intellect seeks to know the true, the will seeks to obtain the good. The intellect acts in the realm of *knowledge*, and the will acts in the realm of *love*. What the will seeks is what the agent loves. In the RSV-CE, this passage from Wisdom reads, "Thou sparest all things, for they are thine, O Lord who *loves* the living." Though this translation lacks the direct implication of will that "wouldst" provides, it is useful in that it speaks of God sparing things because he loves them, which is an act of *will*. In chapter 20, we examine what it means to say, "God is love."

God is indeed the first in order of agents, he acts by intellect and will.

B Every natural agent has a *determinate being*, and acts in accordance with its particular nature. (A rock, for example, falls when dropped, whereas a helium balloon rises.) God, however, is *undetermined* and contains within himself the full perfection of being, so he cannot be compelled to act by necessity of his nature. Instead, "determined effects proceed from his own infinite perfection according to the determination of his will and intellect."

C Every effect proceeds from an agent that causes it insofar as it pre-exists in the agent, since every agent produces its like. (Perhaps a simple example is reproduction in animals, which produce only their like and, even in hybrid species, produce offspring with characteristics that reside in the parents' species.) Now, "since the divine being is his own intellect, effects pre-exist in him after the mode of intellect, and therefore, proceed from him after the same mode." They proceed from him according to the mode of will, since God's inclination to act based on what his intellect conceives belongs to the will. Therefore, not God's nature, but God's will is the cause of things.

5 Does anything cause the divine will?

No. Augustine tells us, "Every efficient cause is greater than the thing effected," and Thomas chimes in that "nothing is greater than the will of God. We must not then seek a cause for it."

Thomas explains that since will follows from the intellect (we will what the intellect understands as good), we can speak of a cause within the person who wills in the same way we speak of a cause within the person who understands. When we reason from known things to unknown things, we understand a premise and a conclusion separately from each other, and the premise acts as the cause of the conclusion that follows from it. But if someone instantly understands the conclusion to be within the premise at the same glance, the premise cannot be said to cause the conclusion, since a thing cannot be its own cause. Still, the thinker would also understand the premise to be the cause of the conclusion.

The same situation applies to the will, for means relate to ends in the same manner that premises relate to conclusions. (The premise can be seen as a means to the end, which is the conclusion.) So if someone separately wills an end or goal in one act, and then wills the means to achieve that end, his willing the end will be the cause of his willing the means. This would not hold for someone who wills both ends and means in the same act, since a thing cannot be its own cause. God, by *one* act (remember, he is pure act and not a series of acts), "understands all things in his essence, so by one act he wills all things to his goodness."

God does not understand effects *because* he understands causes (as we do), since he understands the effect in the cause. So, in his case alone, the will to an end does not cause the will to the means, "yet he wills the ordering of the means to the end. Therefore, he wills this to be as means to that; but does not will this on account of that."

6 *Is God's will always fulfilled?*

Yes. This is among the most important of our questions, since its misunderstanding leads some people away from God or at least from the Church.

How so? Well, to put it in a nutshell, I've known atheists (including myself for a period of twenty-five years) who reasoned something like this: "I'm certainly not perfect, but as a reasonably decent human being, I would never assign people to an everlasting hell for the sins they committed during their limited time on earth, and I would imagine God is a lot nicer than I am. Yet, according to Scripture, hell exists, and the Church teaches us that people who die with mortal sins on their souls will go there. Therefore, if I am to believe that God's will is always fulfilled, I cannot believe what the Church teaches about him or that such a God could exist and be all-good and loving."

There are also other controversial issues, even within our modern Church, that flow from conceptions and misconceptions of just what we mean by the fulfillment of God's will. Let's allow our Angelic Doctor to lift us above the confusion and see the situation most clearly, from the divine perspective.

Thomas starts with Scripture: "God hath done all things, whatsoever he would" (Ps. 113:11). Thomas elaborates later that "since the will of God is the universal cause of all things, it is impossible that the divine will should not produce its effect." Does this mean that God *wills* people to go to hell? This is where a nuanced understanding of God's will is imperative for those who choose to believe in him (or not).

Thomas elaborates that everything that is good, insofar as it is good, is willed by God. Yet we must carefully distinguish between God's *antecedent* and *consequent* wills. God made us good, and indeed, in his image and likeness, through our possession of intellect and will. But with intellect and will come the power to choose whether we will turn toward or away from God.

A good, Thomas tells us, may be changed into the contrary by additional circumstance. For example, that a person should live is good, and that a person should be killed is evil "absolutely considered." Yet, if we add the circumstance that a particular man is a murderer and a threat to society, to kill him can be good, and to allow him to live can be evil. Therefore, we can say of a just judge that *antecedently* (before the circumstance of the murder and persisting danger), the judge wills that the man live, but *consequently* (after the murderous act), he wills that he be hanged. The same applies to God, who antecedently wills that all people will be saved, but consequently wills that some be damned (who have chosen of their free will to commit mortal sin and remain unrepentant). This accords with his divine justice, which we'll examine more fully in chapter 21. In our example of the judge, he would prefer that the murderer live, in that he is a human being, but his killing is just in light of his consequent actions. Thomas tells us that such a qualified will may fittingly be called "a willingness, rather than an absolute will. Thus, it is clear that whatever God wills takes place; although what he wills antecedently may not take place."*

---

* A similar distinction we hear of in our time refers to God's *permissive* will and his *active* will. His *permissive* will refers to what he permits or allows to happen, as opposed to his *active* or *positive* will, which dictates what he wants to happen according to his plan for all of creation. He makes us good and desires our salvation according to his active will, but he allows us, according to his permissive will, to choose evil and forsake heaven. A bit of a brouhaha was stirred in 2019 when the Abu Dhabi document on Human Fraternity, signed by Pope Francis, included the statement that God wills a diversity of religions. Pope Francis later clarified that the statement refers to God's permissive will.

7 Does God's will change?

Some verses in Scripture seem to suggest that it can—for example, "It repenteth me that I made man" (Gen. 6:7).* Thomas replies, however, that such verses are metaphorical, comparing God to *man*, since when we are sorry to have made something, we destroy it, and indeed, we may even destroy something we have made *without a change of will*, as when we make something knowing that it is to be temporary and that we will later disassemble or discard it.

As for possible changeability of *God's* will, Thomas cites a verse that can be interpreted literally: "God is not a man that he should lie, nor as the son of man, that he should be changed" (Num. 23:19).

Thomas tells us that God's will is utterly unchangeable, just as we've seen God and his knowledge and his substance are (Q. 9, a. 1 and Q. 14, a. 15). God's will is at one with his knowledge and essence. Still, Thomas points out an essential distinction: "To change the will is one thing; to will that certain things should be changed is another." God's unchanging will does in fact decree that created things will change and that intellectual agents, like man, can exercise his own, changeable free will. The immutability of God's will limits neither him nor his creatures.

8 Does God's will impose necessity on all things willed?

No, as you may have gathered from our previous questions

---

* The RSV-CE for the complete verse, in clearer modern English, reads, "I will blot out man whom I have created from the face of the ground, man and beast and creeping things and birds of the air, for I am sorry that I have made them."

in this chapter, "The divine will imposes necessity on some things willed, but not all."

God, through his will, is the first cause of all that exists, but through his will he also endows creatures with the power to act as secondary or proximate causal agents (as is seen in the human capacity of free will). What God wills absolutely happens of necessity (absolutely must happen), since "nothing resists the divine will," but what God wills to operate through secondary causes happens contingently, through their causal powers.

9 Does God will evil?

No. You may recall that we touched on this subject in our chapter 2 (Q. 2, a. 3). We saw that since God is the highest good, he will permit evil to exist in his works only if his omnipotence and goodness are such that he can bring goodness even out of evil.

In this article, Thomas makes clear that God does not will evil to be done, and neither does he will that evil not be done, but rather, he *permits* evil to be done. This permissiveness is a good thing in that it allows intellectual creatures to operate as active, moral agents made in God's image with intellect and will. God wills that we possess the capacity to pursue the good and develop virtue, but it is up to us and our wills to determine whether we use our powers to pursue true goods or to fall into vice and sin, by focusing our wills upon evils, or by succumbing to evil by focusing only on partial goods. (Consider the sin of fornication, which possesses merely the partial goodness of physical pleasure while lacking the full goodness of committed love and the bond of matrimony.)

10 Does God have free will?

Yes! Perhaps you already surmised this, since we saw in previous questions in this chapter that God does not will all things of necessity and that nothing causes his will.

Why might someone think otherwise? One objection points to a homily of St. Jerome on the story of the prodigal son, in which he states, "God alone is he who is not liable to sin, nor can he be liable; all others, as having free will, can be inclined to either side." This would suggest that God does not have free will. (A similar teaching you may have heard is that Jesus Christ was like us in all things but sin.)

Thomas begins his reply with a quotation from St. Ambrose, another of the four great original Latin Doctors of the Church (the others being Jerome, Augustine, and Pope Gregory the Great). It goes like this: "The Holy Spirit divideth unto each one as he will, namely, according to the free choice of the will, not in obedience to necessity." It seems likely he was commenting on a verse from St. Paul regarding the Holy Spirit's gifts of special charisms: "All these are inspired by one and the same Spirit, who apportions to each one individually as he wills" (1 Cor. 12:7–11).

Thomas begins by looking at human free will, which we have regarding things that either are not necessary or are not guided by natural instinct. (As for the latter, have you ever tried to keep yourself from blushing when embarrassed or from jumping when you hear a loud crash?) As for the former, we saw before that we do seek the good of our own happiness by necessity, but we have free will in determining the means to attain it. In a similar sense, we can say that God necessarily wills his own goodness, but he has free will with respect to everything else (like every matter pertaining to every created thing). Jerome, St. Thomas tells us, does not deny God's free will, but only his inclination to sin.

11 *Is the will of expression found in God?*

Yes, but what is "the will of expression"? We will flesh it out in its fivefold manner (if I might borrow language characteristic of Thomas), but in short, it means that although God's will is one and is his essence, it is made known to creatures through many expressions, including, for example, *precepts*—rules, instructions, guidelines, like, most famously, the Ten Commandments God gave to Moses. Thomas says that when anyone lays down a precept, it means he wants the precept obeyed. "Hence a divine precept is sometimes called by metaphor the will of God, as in the words: 'thy will be done on earth as it is in heaven'" (Matt. 6:10). (When we read the Ten Commandments or the Sermon on the Mount, for examples, we are reading "the will of God" through revealed expressions.)

12 *Are there five expressions of divine will in God?*

Yes, and they are as follows:

A *Prohibition.* We find many expressions of God's will in Scripture in the form of prohibitions, most notably in the "thou shalt nots" of the Ten Commandments. (This is the only expression that directly relates to evil.)

B *Precepts.* God also informs us of his will in terms of positive acts we must do, such as honoring him in the first three commandments and honoring our parents in the fourth. Of course, Christ defined the greatest precepts of all as to love God with all of our being and our neighbors as ourselves (Matt. 22:35-40; Mark 12:28-34; Luke 10:27, drawing from Deut. 6:4-5 and Lev. 19:18).

C *Counsel.* God's will is expressed through persuasion or advice, as in the Holy Spirit's gift of counsel that supplies us with guidance (Isa. 11:2) or may guide us toward sound human advisers.

D *Operation.* God's will is expressed through his works in the beauty and goodness of visible creation.

E *Permission.* God's will is expressed through permission when he does not impose any obstacles or sanction to an action (as perhaps when we, hopefully having been attentive to God's counsel, choose an honorable vocation in life).

Summa of God's Will

God . . .

1 has will, just as he has intellect.

2 wills his own infinite goodness, and he wills that creatures outside himself share in

3 his goodness.

4 wills only his own good necessarily, but he wills things outside himself as they are ordered to his goodness as their end.

5 causes things through his will.

6 does not will what he does through any cause, for his intellect and will are one.

7 has will that is always fulfilled, but we must distinguish between his *antecedent* will, through which he wills, for example, that all people be saved, and his *consequent* (or permissive) will, in which he allows some people to be damned in accord with the choice of their free will and with divine justice. Thomas calls this "a willingness rather than an absolute will."

8 possesses an unchangeable will that permits creatures to change.

9 imposes necessity on some things, but allows other things to act upon their own wills.

10 does not will evil, though he permits it so that greater good can arise.

11 has free will for all things except that he, of necessity, wills his own goodness.

12 makes his will known through a variety of expressions.

13 expresses his divine will through prohibitions, precepts, counsel, operations, and permission.

20

GOD IS
LOVE

God loves all existing things.

ST, I, Q. 20, a. 2

How does an analysis of *will* pave the way for a treatment of *love*? St. Thomas says that in humans, in the "appetitive part of the soul" (and note that will is also known as the "intellectual appetite"), we find both passions, like love and joy, and also the habits of the moral virtues, like justice and mercy. Therefore, in this chapter, we will examine God's love and touch on his joy, and in the next chapter, we will look at God's justice and mercy. (Thomas saves a detailed explication of God's joy, or *beatitude*, for our last chapter.)

1   *Does love exist in God?*

Yes. This might be a no-brainer, except perhaps for folks who misinterpret the existence of evil to mean that God actively wills it like some kind of sadistic tyrant. Yet, even in Thomas's day, there were some nuanced philosophical objections that cast doubt on whether love could exist in God. We saw in our introductory paragraph that Thomas spoke of love as a passion, and some argued that since God does not have passions, he does not have love. Another argument cited Dionysius, who described love as "a uniting and binding force." God, however, is simple, having no parts to unite or bind!

Thomas begins his response with a clear and literal statement in Scripture: "God is love" (1 John 4:16).

Thomas then argues that God must have love, since we've seen that he has will, and "love is the first movement of the will and of every appetitive faculty." Recall that just as the intellect relates to the *true*, the will relates to the *good*, and as the intellect *knows* the true, the will *loves* the good and tries to obtain and rest in it. As God *is* will, so too *is* he love.

As for our first objection: in human beings composed of body and soul, we do experience passions (desires, aversions, etc.) through the medium of our physical sensations and appetites, but acts of the will, the "intellectual appetite," do not depend upon bodily sensations as the passions do. Therefore, love and joy experienced in the intellect are not passions, and it is in this higher sense that they are in God.

Most interestingly, Thomas calls in not only Scripture, but the pagan Aristotle, who knew based on reason that "God rejoices by an operation that is one and simple." Thomas says it is for this reason that God loves without passion.

Finally, as for our second objection, acts of love do bind and unite toward two things: 1) toward the good we will and 2) toward the person to whom we will it. So, when we love a person, we wish that person good. In this sense, love is a unitive force. This does not contradict God's simplicity, because "the good that he wills for himself is not other than himself, who is good by his essence." God's will also binds others to him in that he wills good to others. Neither does this imply complexity or parts within God.

2   *Does God love all things?*

Yes. An interesting objection to the contrary was based on Dionysius's statement that "love places the lover outside himself, and causes him to pass, as it were, into the object of his love." Does this make sense to you? When we love someone dearly, like a spouse, a parent, or a child, do we not rise above our own selfishness to wish good for him, even if it requires sacrifice and hardship for us? Our love passes, in a sense, from ourselves into that person. Well, we cannot properly say that God passes outside himself into other things, so it would appear that he cannot love other things in the sense that we can.

Consider this brain-twister, too. God's love is eternal, but nothing outside him is eternal, except as it exists in him before he creates it. Yet, what exists within him is none other than himself. Therefore, it would seem, God does not love things outside himself.

And how about a last sample of objections (four were presented in total), not from philosophical analysis, but from revealed Scripture: "Thou hatest all workers of iniquity" (Ps. 5:7). Since nothing can be loved and hated at the same time, God, it would seem, does not love all things.

To the contrary, Thomas cites the wisdom of Wisdom yet again: "Thou lovest all things that are, and hatest none of those things which thou hast made" (Wis. 11:25).

Thomas explains God's love of all things, and how it differs from our love, in a series of logical steps that I'll bullet-point here:

- All existing things are good, since the existence of a thing itself is a good (and the same applies to any perfections an existing thing possesses).

- God's will is the cause of all things.

- Therefore, a thing has existence and good only because it is willed by God.

- To every living thing, God wills some good.

- To love anything is nothing other than to will it good.

- Therefore, it is clear that God loves every existing thing.

The same sequence does not apply to human love because our will is *moved by* the goodness of things but *does not cause* the goodness in those things as God's will does. Indeed, "the love of God infuses and creates goodness."

As for the objections, Dionysius himself eloquently explains that "he himself, the cause of all things, by his abounding love and goodness, is placed outside himself by his providence for all existing things."

As for the second objection based on the eternity of God's love: even before things exist on their own, God has known them in their proper natures and loved them, in a similar way to which we, through images in our minds, know things that exist in themselves. I can't help but recall a scriptural verse here, too: "Before I formed you in the womb, I knew you" (Jer. 1:5).

Finally, as for God hating workers of iniquity (or the bloodthirsty and deceitful, depending on your Bible translation), Thomas tells us that nothing prevents us from loving something according to one aspect and hating it according to another. God loves all sinners *in that they exist* and have their existence from him, but he does not love them *in that they are sinners*, for under that aspect "they have not existence at all, but fall short of it; and this in them is not from God. Hence, under this aspect, they are hated by him." (Perhaps this will recall the famous admonishment for us to "love the sinner but hate the sin."*)

3 Does God love all things equally?

No. And yet, we do read passages like this one: "He hath equally care of all" (Wis. 6:8).

---

* As for the origins of this phrase, Fr. Vincent Serpa, O.P. has provided the following: it's from St. Augustine. His Letter 211 (c. 424) contains the phrase *cum dilectione hominum et odio vitiorum*, which translates roughly to "with love for mankind and hatred of sins." The phrase has become more famous as "love the sinner but hate the sin" or "hate the sin and not the sinner" (the latter form appearing in Mohandas Gandhi's 1929 autobiography). See https://www.catholic.com/qa/who-said-love-the-sinner-hate-the-sin.

Thomas starts his explanation with a beautiful passage from Augustine: "God loves all things that he has made, and among them rational creatures more, and of these especially those who are members of his only-begotten Son; and much more than all, his only-begotten Son himself."

Thomas elaborates that God loves all things equally "on the part of the act of the will itself, which is more or less intense." God's will is simple and always the same. Yet, "on the part of the good itself that a person wills for the beloved," we are said to love one more than another, in wishing them greater good, and this is also found in God. God is the cause of goodness, and some things are clearly better than others, possessing higher perfections. In this sense we can say that God loves inanimate objects less than plants, plants less than animals, and animals less than man—and, as Augustine adds, those who do not follow Christ less than those who do, and finally, even believers in Christ less than Christ himself.

As for the verse from Wisdom, Thomas tells us God is said to care equally for everything, not because he bestows equal good on all things, "but because he administers all things with a like wisdom and goodness."

4 Does God always love better things more?

Yes, as you might have surmised from our last question and answer. There are some interesting objections. Augustine just told us (and Thomas agreed) that God loves Christ most of all, yet we read this: "'He spared not his own Son, but delivered him up for us all' (Rom. 8:32). Therefore God does not always love more the better things."

Further, Scripture says of man, "Thou hast made him a

little less than the angels" (Ps. 8:6). Yet we read in Hebrews 2:16, "Nowhere doth he take hold of angels, but of the seed of Abraham he hath taken hold."* Therefore, it would appear, that since angels are better than man, God does not always love better things more.

Thomas responds with an intriguing scriptural verse: "Every beast loveth its like" (Ecclus. 13:19). The better a thing is, the more it is like God, and thus the more God loves it. Better things have received more good things through God's divine will, and "God's loving one thing more than another is else than his willing for that thing a greater good." God's will causes goodness in things. Some things are better than others because he has willed them a greater good and, hence, loves them more. Therefore, God loves better things more.

And perhaps we should recall an earlier lesson that we encountered in chapter 12, Q. 6 on God's knowability: that whoever among us embraces God's offer of love most fully on earth will experience the bliss of seeing his essence most fully in heaven.

Summa of God's Love

God . . .

1 is love as he is will, love being the first movement of will.

2 loves all things (which exist because of his love).

3 loves some things more than others.

4 loves better things more than lesser things.

---

* This reads in the RSV-CE, "For surely it is not with angels that he is concerned, but with the descendants of Abraham."

21

GOD'S JUSTICE AND
MERCY

God acts mercifully, not indeed
by going against his justice, but by doing
something more than justice.

ST, I, Q. 21, a. 3

According to St. Thomas, regarding what follows consideration of God's will, first comes love, then comes—justice and mercy. Is God just? Is he merciful? Is it possible that he is both at once? Let's find out.

1 *Is God just?*

Yes. Why might you think he's not? Well, justice is fundamentally a matter of paying another his rightful due. But God owes no man anything. So how can we say he is just?

Scripture tells us plainly in Psalm 10:8, "The Lord is just, and hath loved justice."

Thomas begins by elaborating that there are two forms of justice: *commutative* justice and *distributive* justice. (Thomas treats the virtue of justice in all of its forms and ramifications in great detail later in the *Summa*, devoting over 250 pages to it in II-II, Qs. 57-120. It is marvelous material for those of us who would hope to be just in our acts, as God is.)

Anyway, here are the two forms in brief:

- *Commutative justice.* This form of justice consists of one-on-one interactions of giving and receiving among private individuals, as in business transactions.

- *Distributive justice.* This form of justice involves distribution. The *Catechism* says it "regulates what the community owes its citizens in proportion to their contributions and needs" (2411). Further, we are called to exercise both forms of justice, both in our one-on-one interactions and as members of groups or societies. For "without commutative justice, no other form of justice is possible."

Still, Thomas tells us that commutative justice does not apply to God. St. Paul asks, "Who hath first given to him, and recompense shall be made him?" (Rom. 11:35).* As our objection holds, God does indeed owe nothing to any man. He stands in no one's debt.†

Still, God is indeed completely just in the distributive sense that applies to him. Thomas gives an example from his time of distributive justice: a good ruler or steward who justly distributes to each person what he has merited. Well, God is the just ruler of the entire universe, fairly distributing a universe of goods. In the words of Dionysius, we see that God is truly just "in seeing how he gives to all existing things what is proper to the condition of each and preserves the nature of each one in the order and with the powers that properly belong to it."

2   *Is God's justice truth?*

Yes. This one may seem abstruse, so I'll try to do it justice. Objections holding that the justice of God is *not* truth arise from the fact that justice resides in the will, and Aristotle has noted that truth resides in the intellect. Hence,

---

* This reads in the RSV-CE, perhaps more clearly, "Or who has given a gift to him that he might be repaid?"

† Later in the *Summa* (II-II, Q. 81), when addressing the virtue of religion as it relates to justice, Thomas looks at this fact from the human perspective. We can never exercise full justice in our relations with God. True justice is giving another his rightful due *in equal measure*. God gave us our existence, and this we can never fully repay. Through the allied virtue of *religion*, however, we repay to the extent that we are able through honoring and worshipping him through internal acts like prayer and external acts like adoration, sacrifice, and tithing. Recall as well the words said at Mass during the Eucharistic prayer: "Let us give thanks to the Lord our God," to which the response is "it is right and just."

truth and justice are two different things. Further, Aristotle has described truth and justice as two separate virtues (and Thomas himself does so as well later in the *Summa*: II-II, Qs. 58 and 109).

And yet we read this in the Psalms: "'Mercy and truth have met each other,' where truth stands for justice" (Ps. 84:11).

Truth, as you will recall, means the equation or conformity of mind with thing. So, when we make a statement about some external thing, our statement is true or false depending on whether our conception equates with the thing. But for situations in which our minds are the rules or measures of things, truth depends on whether the thing corresponds to our conception, as when an artist or craftsman judges whether or not his product is truly what he had intended.

Now, just how works of art are related to the art of the artist, "so are works of justice related to the law with which they accord." Therefore, God's justice, which establishes the order of things in accordance with the rule of his wisdom— that is, the law of his justice—"is suitably called truth. Thus, we also in human affairs speak of the truth of justice."

As for truth residing in the intellect and justice in the will, the law that governs justly resides in the intellect, and the command whereby just actions are performed according to the law resides in the will. (Justice is not either/or, but both/and in relation to intellect and will.)

Finally, as for the differing virtues of truth and justice that Aristotle (and later Thomas) describe, the Philosopher and the Angelic Doctor, in describing truth as a virtue, refer specifically to that "whereby a man shows himself in word and deed such as he really is." It consists in the conformity of signs (words) with things (actions). We might say in modern language that the person with the virtue of truth "walks his talk," is honest, has integrity—the opposite of a hypocrite, a liar, or a con man. The person with the virtue of justice shows conformity of words and deeds with just laws or rules.

3 Is God merciful?

Yes—thanks be to God! Some argued that mercy could not rightly be attributed to God, arguing, for example, based on St. John Damascene's observation that mercy is a kind of sorrow, and there is no sorrow in God, so there can be no mercy, either.

Another argument defined mercy as a relaxation of judgment and cited this scriptural verse: "If we believe not, he continueth faithful; he cannot deny himself" (2 Tim. 2:13). God would not deny himself or his words, so he would not remit what his justice has demanded.

Thomas counters with clear words from Scripture: "He is a merciful and gracious Lord" (Ps. 110:4). He explains that mercy is indeed rightly attributed to God, in its *effect*, though not as an affection of *passion*.

The connection between mercy and sorrow is based on the Latin word *misericordia* for mercy, which means a misery or sadness of the *cor* (heart). The person *feeling* merciful (i.e., experiencing the *passion* of mercy) treats another's misery as if it were his own. The *actions* the merciful person takes to overcome the other person's misery relate to the *effects* of mercy.

Now, God himself does not experience sorrow or misery, but he most certainly takes action to dispel people's misery. Consider that misery can be seen as a defect in a person, in that he lacks the goodness of happiness proper to him. Defects in goodness can be removed only by the perfection of some kind of goodness, "and the primary source is God." Indeed, God bestows perfections not only according to his divine goodness, but also according to his justice, liberality, and mercy under different aspects. Let's see how:

- God bestows perfections, *in their absolute sense*, according to his *goodness*, as we saw in Q. 6, aa. 1 and 4, addressing the goodness in God.

- God bestows perfections to things *in their proper proportions* according to his *justice*.

- God bestows perfections to things, *not for his own use*, but only because of his goodness and because of his *liberality* (he bestows such things freely and generously).

- God bestows perfections to *remove defects* according to his *mercy*.

Truly, God is good, just, generous, and merciful!

As for the objection that mercy relaxes and somehow contradicts justice, Thomas states clearly, "God acts mercifully, not indeed by going against his justice, but by doing something more than justice." It's like when a man who owes another man a hundred dollars pays him two hundred instead. That is not an act against justice, but an act that adds liberality or mercy. In a similar vein, if we forgive someone who has injured us, it is as though we had given him a gift. Indeed, we have been instructed to do so: "Forgive one another, as Christ has forgiven you" (Eph. 4:32).

In short, mercy does not contradict or destroy justice, but fulfills it. Thus, we read, "Mercy exalteth itself above judgment" (James 2:13). God is both just and merciful.

4 Are justice and mercy in every work of God?

Yes, though it might appear not. Indeed, in the same verse from James we just saw cited, we also read about "judgment without mercy in him that hath not done mercy." It would appear, then, that not every work of God contains justice and mercy.

Thomas begins with this scriptural verse: "All the ways of the Lord are mercy and truth" (Ps. 24:10). He then elaborates that both mercy and truth are indeed found in all of God's acts. Recall that mercy removes "defects" (e.g., flaws, imperfections, impairments, impediments) of any kind. Still, the only defects that can rightly be classified as a misery (bearing upon mercy) are found within rational beings whose nature is to be happy (rather than miserable). That rational beings, or any beings, exist at all is due to God's *wisdom* and *goodness*. Further, whatever God does to created things according to the proper order and proportion befitting them belongs to his *justice*. So justice must be in all of God's works. But note that *divine justice always presupposes divine mercy and is founded upon it.* Creatures are owed nothing by God, yet God bestows perfections upon them that remedy their defects or imperfections. He gives them more than they are due, more than what is proportionate to their merits, and this exceeds justice alone, but is due to God's mercy.

As for the statement from James regarding judgment without mercy for those who have been unmerciful, Thomas says that although justice and mercy are found in all of God's works, in some works justice "appears more forcibly," and in other works, mercy stands out. Indeed, even those lacking mercy who are justly damned (as James describes) receive some measure of mercy from God in that their punishment falls short of what they truly deserve in willfully turning away from God, who has given them all that they are.*

Summa of God's Justice and Mercy

God . . .

1 is just, distributing to all things perfections in due proportions.

2 is both justice and truth, in will and in intellect.

3 is merciful, remedying defects in all created things in the fulfillment of justice.

4 is both just and merciful in all his works.

---

* For those who find this idea intriguing, Thomas spells it out in some detail in five articles in the Supplement to the *Summa*, Q. 99, "On God's Mercy and Justice Toward the Damned." I summarized and commented on it myself in chapter 37 of *Aquinas on the Four Last Things* (Sophia Institute Press, 2021).

22

GOD'S
PROVIDENCE

Divine providence imposes necessity upon some
things—not upon all, as some formerly believed.

ST, I, Q. 22, a. 4

After having considered what relates to God's will absolutely, St. Thomas tells us we will move on to consider what
relates to both the intellect and will, first off being God's
providence in relation to all created things. After the moral
virtues—fortitude, temperance, justice, etc.—comes the
consideration of the virtue of prudence that guides them. In
the same way, providence comes next in the consideration of
the acts of God's will that guide the universe.

❶ *Can we rightly attribute providence to God?*

Yes. One interesting argument that might make us think otherwise is based on sound moral analysis of the great pagan philosophers Cicero and Aristotle. Cicero, in defining the virtue of prudence (or practical wisdom), listed *providentia*, providence, from the Latin *pro* meaning to come before and *visio* for vision, as one of its essential parts.* Yet prudence, according to Aristotle, includes *eubolia*, taking good counsel.† God never has any doubts for which he needs to take counsel, so prudence and providence "cannot belong to God."

Thomas knew well, however, that it is written: "But thou, Father, governest all things by providence" (Wis. 14:3). God not only gives *existence* to everything he creates, but creates them so they are *ordered toward him* as their final end or goal. Now, God is the cause of all things, the *type* (or form) of effects pre-exists God's intellect, and *the type of the order of*

---

* Here, as in many other passages we've seen, Thomas mentions in passing teachings he will explicate in great detail later in the *Summa*. In brief, Cicero defined three essential "parts" of prudence as memory, understanding, and foresight (or providence), which St. Albert the Great, Thomas's teacher, incorporated in his own analysis of prudence, for to achieve the virtues' goals (requiring *providence* or *foresight* of what will work) we must act in the present (based on our *understanding* of moral laws and particular situations), guided by the *memory* of moral lessons and practical experiences. In Thomas's own analysis of prudence in *ST*, II-II, Q. 48, he incorporates those same three "parts" from Cicero, as well as parts from Aristotle and the philosophers Plotinus and Macrobius, yielding eight "integral parts" of prudence, being memory, understanding, docility, shrewdness, reason, foresight, circumspection, and caution.

† Indeed, in describing "potential" or "allied" parts or virtues that serve prudence, Thomas includes Aristotle's *eubolia*, along with *synesis*, which judges among ethical alternatives, and *gnome*, which casts wise practical judgment in extreme or unusual cases—as perhaps when King Solomon suggested cleaving in twain the baby of two women claiming to be its mother (1 Kings 3:16–18)!

things toward their last end also exists in the divine mind, and *this is what is meant by providence.* In considering the three main parts of prudence, remembrance of the past and understanding of the present serve to determine how we will act in the future to obtain the proper end. Therefore, providence—foresight regarding attainment of the goal—is the chief part of prudence, which memory and understanding serve.

In God, there is nothing ordered to an end, since he is the last end. *The fact that all created things are ordered to God as the last end is what we call God's providence.* As Boethius states, "Providence is the divine type itself, seated in the Supreme Ruler, which disposeth all things."

True, God does not seek any counsel outside himself since his knowledge is total and certain, but it is he in whom others seek counsel: "Who worketh all things according to the counsel of his will" (Eph. 1:11). God's providential plan is overseen and carried out through his divine government of all that is.

2 *Is everything subject to God's providence?*

Yes. This question has been a subject of great importance, from long before Thomas's time, even unto our own (and it doesn't take too much foresight to predict that it will remain a controversial issue). So it warrants analysis in quite some detail. Hence, we will peruse all five objections, as well as Thomas's replies.

A Some argued that not everything happens due to divine providence, since nothing foreseen can happen by chance. It would mean there is no such thing as *chance* or *luck*.

B A wise caretaker protects any under his charge from any *defects* or *evils*, as far as is within his power. Yet we see many evils all around us. So either God cannot stop these evils and is not all-powerful, or he is all-powerful but does not exert his power to care for everything.

C Aristotle declares that "prudence is the right reason of things contingent concerning which there are counsel and choice." But many things happen from *necessity* (as by the laws of nature, we might say) without reasoned *choice*. Therefore, not everything is subject to God's providence.

D Whatever is *left to itself* is not a matter of providence, yet we read this in Scripture: "God made man from the beginning, and left him in the hand of his own counsel" (Ecclus. 15:14). Further, "I let them go according to the desires of their heart" (Ps. 80:13).

E Finally, the apostle Paul tells us, "God doth not care for oxen" (1 Cor. 9:9). Certainly God's *lack of care* would apply to other irrational creatures. Therefore, not everything is under God's providence.

As for Thomas's scriptural rejoinder, we read this of divine wisdom: "She reacheth from end to end mightily, and ordereth all things sweetly" (Wis. 8:1).

Thomas then moves into some interesting ideas in the history of philosophy, noting that philosophers such as Democritus (fifth century B.C.) argued that there was no divine providence, since the universe was made merely by chance. This is sometimes referred to as Democritus's *atomic theory*, proposed millennia before physicists discovered what we today call the atom. Democritus argued that everything in the universe is made up of invisibly small atoms that bounce around and unite by random processes. Indeed, six centuries later, as we saw much earlier in this book, the Stoic philosopher and Roman emperor Marcus Aurelius would refer to the great dilemma of the nature of the universe time and again as either "providence or atoms."

Of even more relevance, many modern atheists in our own time reject the idea of God's providence, siding with chance: arguing that man himself was not created in God's image and likeness but arose through chance events, starting at the atomic level and working their way up through organic chemical compounds, primitive life forms, and finally evolving, through chance mutations and natural selection, into man, with no role whatever for God and his providence. (See why the question is of such importance?)

Thomas continues by telling us that others thought God's providence does exist, but extends only to heavenly or celestial beings. This view is expressed in this line from Eliphaz the Temanite in the book of Job: "The clouds are his cover; and he doth not consider our things; and he walketh about the poles of heavens" (Job 22:14). He notes too that Rabbi Moses (Maimonides, twelfth century) extended God's care to humans, since we have intellectual, spiritual souls, but believed that God's providence does not extend to lower beings.

Thomas argues, to the contrary, that all things that exist are indeed subject to God's providence, both in general and as particular individual beings. As we saw, everything acts according to its own nature, for the final end to which it is ordered, that final end being God. God knows, orders, oversees, and governs the entire universe and every individual thing within it. As St. Paul has told us, "Those things that are of God are well ordered" (Rom. 13:1).

Let's clear things up further by looking at Thomas's replies to each objection:

A Regarding events of chance or luck, such events appear so to those who do not see all of the causal factors at work. What seems to happen for no particular reason to us is still a part of God's overall plan. (I'm reminded of a friend who calls coincidences "God-incidences.") Thomas uses the example of two servants who seem to meet somewhere by chance who are unaware that their master had planned their meeting in advance and sent them there on purpose. Another example that comes to my mind might be a single man and woman who seem to meet by chance, not realizing that mutual friends planned to invite them to some outing just so such a meeting would happen "by chance." Those of us who are married might think about how and where we met our spouses. Chances are (so to speak!) most of us were not purposely set up by friends, but all of us "happened to" meet that loving spouse in accordance with God's divine providence!

B The "problem of evil" has reared its ancient head again. Well, let's consider the case of a human caretaker who must overlook a multitude of things—let's call it a gardener who tends to a vast estate. He will do his best to care for every single flower or tree, as best he can, but sometimes he may allow some diseased plant to die off, or even remove it, for the sake of the garden as a whole. In a broader sense, the fact that some *particular* individual things may suffer defects contrary to their particular nature may serve the plan of *universal* nature. Perhaps our dead plant will even be composted to nourish the surviving plants. Now, if we extend the gardener's garden to God's entire universe, we will see that God, though indeed all-powerful, does allow certain defects to exist in particular things so that greater good can come from them, according to his providential plan, "for if all evil was prevented, much good would be absent from the universe." (Thinking here from a parent's perspective, how wise and caring would we be if we never allowed our children to stumble, to scrape a knee, or make mistakes, or suffer minor evils of various sorts, so they could learn from them and grow better?)

C As for prudence (and providence) and the distinction between things happening by choice and by necessity, Thomas states quite nicely that "man is not the author of nature," hence our prudence and providence are far more limited than those of God! Man's providence uses and makes choices regarding natural things as they are in their nature by necessity, but since God gives things their nature, his providence is not limited like ours. Democritus (and his modern-day followers) erringly attributes necessity to atoms themselves, rather than to him who created them.

D As for God leaving some things up to us and our choices, this does not mean humans are exempt from God's providence, but that we are endowed with choice and have no fixed nature that determines us toward one particular course of action (like an unsupported rock that must fall to the earth). Our ability to refer to our "own counsel" and the "desires of our own hearts"—that is, our *free will*—is itself "traced to God as a cause," so that even acts of human free will "must be subject to divine providence," falling within the orbit and order of God's master plan for the universe. This does not deny the causal reality of our free will, but reminds us that this power comes to us from God.

E Finally, as to God not caring for oxen (a sad thought, perhaps?), we have seen that God loves all existing creatures, although some more than others. Thomas says the verse simply means that our human free will renders us subject to God's providence in a way that animals are not subject to it. Their actions do not constitute faults or merits (springing neither from vice nor from virtue, but from natural instincts) and do not result in punishment or reward as do our actions. Still, God does care for oxen. All irrational creatures exist under his divine providence, though not in the same way that humans do.

3 Does God have immediate providence over everything?

Yes. Some thought God did not exercise immediate governance over all of creation, for various reasons. Consider, for example, that a king, in keeping with his dignity, does not carry out every act of governance, but assigns ministers to handle things for him to provide for his subjects. God is infinitely more dignified and powerful than an earthly king and would not directly involve himself in immediate providence over all things.

Another interesting argument cited Augustine, who wrote, "It is better to be ignorant of some things than to know them, for example, vile things," and Thomas noted that Aristotle said the same thing.* Therefore, it would seem that God would not direct his providence over "bad and vile things."

To the contrary, Thomas begins with this verse from Scripture: "What other hath he appointed over the earth or whom hath he set over the world which he made?" (Job. 34:13). He notes as well that Gregory the Great had commented on the verse as follows: "Himself he ruleth the world which he himself hath made."

An interesting feature of Thomas's own answer is his description of a threefold or three-tiered providence espoused by Plato, according to writings of Gregory of Nyssa and Augustine. This theory held first that the supreme deity held immediate providence over all spiritual beings. Second was providence over beings that can be generated or corrupted, and this was exercised not by God, but by multiple "divinities" who circulate in the heavens (e.g., the planets). At the third tier of providence over human affairs, he assigned demons, per Augustine.

Thomas saw that this was an erroneous view and provided a two-tiered alternative. He said providence involves two things: "The type of the order of things foreordained

---

* Here is yet another example of where Thomas briefly describes a principle relevant to a particular topic in relation to God that he fleshes out in great detail later in the *Summa*, where he discusses human nature. In this case, in II-II, Q. 167, he explains the vice of *curiositas* (curiosity), through which we care too much about vile or unimportant things, and in Q. 166, he explains the virtue of *studiositas* (studiousness), through which we focus our attention on the things that matter most.

toward an end; and the execution of this order, which is called government." As regards the first, God does exercise immediate providence over every single thing that exists. His intellect contains the type or form of every existing thing, no matter how small or seemingly insignificant (for all things pre-exist within God's intellect). As for the second aspect of providence regarding execution or government: God, in perfect accord with his dignity, does delegate his authority to intermediaries so that superior, more perfect beings can govern inferior, less perfect beings. In this way, he shares his goodness in that "the dignity of causality is imparted even to creatures." *We* indeed are called (and honored) to be ministers of God's will here on earth.

Come to think of it, Jesus taught us to pray, "Thy will be done on earth, as it is in heaven" (Matt. 6:10), and Thomas, when commenting elsewhere on this, the third petition of the "Our Father" prayer, notes it means we pray "that his will be fulfilled in us."[10] We have our own role to play as causal agents with the grand plan of God's providence.

As for the idea that God would not attend to evil or vile things, Thomas says it is better for humans not to learn about low and vile things at the expense of accruing knowledge about better and higher things, since we cannot understand many things at once and because knowledge of evil things may pervert our wills and lead us toward evil. God, to the contrary, knows everything simultaneously "at one glance," and his will can never turn toward evil.

4 Does providence necessarily cause the things foreseen?

No, and this is an important question because, though Thomas does not use the term, it relates to a theory popular even in our day known as *determinism*. Here is a modern definition from Merriam-Webster: "a theory or doctrine that acts of the will, occurrences in nature, or social or psychological phenomena are causally determined by preceding events or natural laws."

Many modern determinists, being materialists or "atomists," as we saw before, believe that everything happens of necessity, including acts that seem to come from human free will, because we could theoretically trace back every thought and desire to the massive chain of random physical causes and events that have occurred over the course of time. (And if that truly were the case, they would have to admit that even their belief in determinism was determined by forces outside their control and not through rational processes and choices of the will, free will being considered a popular delusion.)

In Thomas's day, some argued against the idea of free will, not because of materialistic determinism, but because of God's providence. One objection offered this quotation from Boethius: "Fate from the immutable source of providence binds together human acts and fortunes by the indissoluble connect of causes." Therefore, it is argued, providence imposes necessity on all things that are foreseen.

Thomas clarifies the matter by explaining that providence imposes necessity only on some things, but not on all things, as some people have supposed. The secondary causal powers found in created things operate according to the natures God gave them. Hence, unless something else intervenes (like water, in this case), dry kindling tossed in a raging fire will, *of necessity*, burn, as is the case with the necessity of innumerable cause-and-effect relationships we see in nature. Still, even some natural processes act only *contingently*.

Msgr. Glenn provides the example of a seed that may produce a plant, but only if it lands in the proper soil, with the proper amount of water, nutrients, sunlight, etc.[11] As for human beings, our freely chosen acts (as opposed to reflexive actions like a sneeze or digestive processes that go on without our conscious direction) are contingent upon the choices we make. Providence does not hamper man's free will.

The twentieth-century comedian Flip Wilson's character Geraldine was famous for exclaiming, "The devil made me do it!" whenever she did something wrong. Thomas would disagree, noting that not even God in his divine providence makes us do the things we choose to do!

Summa of God's Providence

God's providence . . .

1 oversees, guides, and governs all created things, directing them toward him as their end.

2 is exercised over every single thing, but in different ways for different things, depending on their natures.

3 operates immediately and directly in everything as the primary cause of his governance; but he grants creatures the power to act as secondary causes in the administration of his plan for the order of creation.

4 imposes necessity on some things, and is contingent for other things, most remarkably for human actions, for his providence does not hinder the use of the free will he granted as essential to our nature.

23

GOD AND
PREDESTINATION

It is fitting that God should predestine men.
For all things are subject to his providence.

ST, I, Q. 23, a. 1

St. Thomas tells us that after treating of providence, we must turn to predestination. It appears that Merriam-Webster would agree. We examined their primary definition of *determinism* in our last chapter on providence. Their second (option b) definition of determinism is "a belief in predestination."

Well, this is a hot topic among believers and non-believers, even in our day. I know this well myself: in 2019, during a Q&A after a talk on the Stoic philosophers, a questioner, knowing I am Catholic, asked how I would reconcile the concept of free will with the Catholic concept of predestination.

Some people are put off by the idea that predestination means that God has created some people in order that they could suffer for eternity someday in hell, and there's nothing they can do about it. Some fundamentalists of certain Protestant denominations, especially Calvinists, believe just this. (The believers I have known personally have tended to consider themselves among the chosen "elect" on their way to heaven.) As for Catholics, let's see what the Angelic Doctor has to say about this important and often confusing doctrine.

1 Are people predestined by God?

Yes, but it is vitally important that we clarify just what is meant by *predestination*. The first and most detailed objection should help us get to the gist of it. This objection held that people are not predestined by God, citing this passage from St. John Damascene: "It must be borne in mind that God foreknows but does not predetermine everything, since he foreknows all that is in us but does not predetermine it all." God made humans as masters of our own acts through our free will, and therefore, merit and demerit are in us. Merit and demerit are not predestined, which does away with the idea of predestination.

Thomas rejoins to the contrary with this scriptural passage: "Whom he predestined, he also called" (Rom. 8:30). He continues that it is fitting for God to predestine human beings, since all things are subject to his providence, as we have just seen. Recall, though, that the end toward which God directs things is twofold. The end that exceeds natural human capacity is to see God in his essence in heaven while experiencing eternal life. (We examined how we cannot see God in his essence by any natural power in chapter 12, Q. 4.) The other end is attainable through creatures' natural powers, and this is to operate within God's ordering of the universe in accord with the creature's nature.

When it comes to ends that exceed a creature's natural power, the creature must be directed, as "an arrow is directed by the archer toward a mark." So "a rational being capable of eternal life is led toward it, directed, as it were, by God." This is because the direction pre-exists in God as the type or form of the order of all things toward an end, as we saw when examining providence.

Now (and this is crucial), "the type in the mind of the doer of something to be done is a kind of pre-existence in him of the thing to be done"—like the idea of a house within the mind of a builder. Therefore, "*the type of the aforesaid direction of a rational creature is called predestination.*" For to destine is to direct or send. Thus, it is clear that predestination, as regards its objects, is a part of providence.

As regards the passage from John Damascene, Thomas says he is referring to natural things that are, of necessity, *predetermined* to one end, and not to rational beings, who are predestined but not predetermined toward one end. Thomas points out that we can see this is the case because Damascene adds this line: "He does not will malice, nor does he compel virtue."

Note Damascene's use of "predetermine" (*praedetermino* in the Latin) and not "predestination" (*praedestinatio*). The two, though often confused, are not the same! God *predestines* human beings toward him as their end, but he does not *predetermine* whether or not we will attain him.

Msgr. Glenn provides a helpful summary of the matter: "Providence disposing the supernatural means by which a man gets to heaven is called predestination." In other words, God has established in the order of creation that human beings cannot attain eternal life with him without his supernatural aid or grace, and it's up to us to what extent we choose to accept or reject it.

2   Does predestination place something within the predestined?

No. Some have thought there must be some kind of mark or character within the predestined. One argument cited Augustine's statement that predestination is the preparation of God's benefits. Preparation, it was argued, is something in the thing prepared. (Sorry, but the first example that comes to my mind is marinating a piece of steak in preparation to cook it.) Therefore, it would seem, "predestination is something in the predestined."

Thomas rejoins with another of Augustine's teachings: "Predestination is the foreknowledge of God's benefits." Foreknowledge (or providence) exist not in the things known, but in their knower. Predestination, therefore, is in God, who predestines, and not in predestined creatures.

3   Does God reprobate anyone?

Yes, and this one is nuanced, to be sure. To begin to unpack it, we should define *reprobatio* (reprobation). By *reprobation*

Thomas means the condemnation of persons to eternal damnation; the opposite of predestination, by which persons are rewarded with eternal life.

Although we have seen that God loves all things that are and hates none (Wis. 11:25), we also read that God declared, "I have loved Jacob but have hated Esau" (Mal. 1:2, 3). How do we resolve this paradox?

Thomas notes that according to divine providence, people are ordained (ordered or directed) toward eternal life with God as their end, but God's providence also *permits* some people to fall away from their ordained end through the choices of their own free will. As *predestination* is part of providence regarding those who attain eternal life, *reprobation* is part of providence regarding those who turn aside from that eternal end. Both imply not only foreknowledge (or providence), but "something more." Neither of these is *predetermined*. That "something more" reflects the choices of a person's free will—whether God's freely offered graces are accepted or rejected in favor of sin.

God did not hate Esau in the sense that he created him so he could go to hell. He loved him as he loves all people, but he reprobated Esau because of the sinful actions Esau chose while alive on earth, thus rejecting the eternal life God had offered him.*

---

* There are other interpretations of Malachi 1:2 and 3 (also cited by Paul in Rom. 9:3) that suggest that the statement that God "hated" Esau means only, in the Semitic expression of the time, that he loved him less than Jacob, and that this verse does not necessarily mean that Esau must be in hell. See, for example, Tom Nash, "Are Some Destined to Be Damned?" Oct. 25, 2018, https://www.catholic.com/magazine/online-edition/are-some-destined-to-be-damned. The Church teaches that only unrepentant sinners who die with mortal sins on their souls will have chosen to spend eternity in hell (CCC 1861).

4 Does God choose the predestined?

Yes. Those who go to heaven can appropriately be called the *chosen* or *elect*. Some disagreed, however, arguing, for example, that election implies some kind of discrimination among persons, but "God wills all men to be saved" (1 Tim. 2:4).

Thomas first counters with another verse from St. Paul: "He chose us in him before the foundation of the world" (Eph. 1:4). God loves all people, and he elects (chooses) for eternal life those who accept his grace. Thomas's explanation of the quotation from the letter to Timothy bears repeating in full (bearing in mind our previous discussion regarding God's will in chapter 19): "God wills all men to be saved by his antecedent will, which is to will not simply, but relatively; and not by his consequent will, which is to will simply."

Hopefully every loving parent can see the sense of this in relation to this life on earth. We will "antecedently" that our own children be happy, live virtuous lives, and love God as adults, but even if we had the power, we would not will it "simply" by forcing them to live out the choices *we* make for them. Instead, we give them counsel, direction, and hopefully good example, while letting them make their own choices in life as rational beings with their own free will, even if for the worse.

5 Does God's foreknowledge of merits cause predestination?

No. We are predestined to eternal life *not* because God knows *we* will live meritorious lives. We are not the cause of our own salvation. We do not climb to heaven by pulling on our own bootstraps. As Paul has written, "Not by the works of justice which we have done, but according to his mercy he saved us" (Titus 3:5).

Thomas explains that to say God saves us means that he predestined us that we should be saved. Therefore, foreknowledge of our merits is not what predestines us to heaven.

We won't dig too deep into the history of the heretical or near-heretical weeds Thomas debunks in this article, but it may be of interest and help to mention that some people believed, based on some writings of Origen, that predestination is based on merits people accrued in a former life, before they were united to bodies in this life. Paul, however, makes clear that this is erroneous: "For when they were not yet born, nor had done any good or evil . . . not of works, but of him that calleth, it was said to her, 'The elder shall serve the younger'" (Rom. 9:11, 12).

Another view, called *Pelagianism* (named after the fourth- and fifth-century theologian Pelagius), espoused what some liken to "lifting ourselves up by our own bootstraps." Pelagius taught that meritorious acts come first from us, and then God rewards us in heaven. In essence, he taught that we can attain heaven simply through our own efforts, and perhaps with the aid of virtuous companions, but *without the need for God's grace*. Thomas says Paul also made clear that this view is in error: "We are not sufficient to think anything of ourselves as of ourselves" (2 Cor. 3:5). No principle of actions within us comes prior to our thinking. Therefore, nothing that begins within us can be the cause of predestination.

It is God's grace that both *disposes* or *prepares us* for the salvation that leads to heaven and *aids us* in our efforts to attain it.

6 *Is predestination certain?*

Yes! (I dare say, "Certainly!") But some thought that perhaps it isn't. We are warned, for example, to "hold that which thou hast, that no one take thy crown" (Apoc. 3:11). Therefore, it seems, we cannot be certain of our predestined heavenly crown.

Thomas responds with a medieval gloss on Romans 8:29, which reads in part, "Whom he foreknew, he also predestinated." The gloss reads, "Predestination is the foreknowledge and preparation for the benefits of God, by which whosoever are freed will most certainly be free."

Thomas clarifies that predestination "certainly and most infallibly" does take effect, yet (and this is of extreme importance) "it does not impose any necessity, so that namely, its effect should take place of necessity." If I might interject a modern analogy, God has not created us as pre-programmed robots whose every action must follow their programming. His providence and the workings of predestination factor in our own causal power as moral agents with wills of our own. Whoever cooperates with God's will that we be saved will be saved and receive his heavenly crown. Of this we can be sure. Whoever rejects God's antecedent will and chooses to perform mortal sin will lose that heavenly crown.* This is certain, too.

7 *Is there a certain number of predestined persons?*

Yes. Augustine said, "The number of the predestined is certain and can neither be increased or diminished." Some

---

* Thomas, being Thomas, elaborates further on just about every topic somewhere in his writings. If you would like to learn more about heavenly crowns, see *ST*, Supplement, Q. 96, "Of the Aureoles."

religious groups in our day believe that the number is certain—and that they know it!

If I might digress on this issue (which also taps into the importance of knowing when Scripture is to be read literally and when to be read figuratively), in Revelation 7:1-8, 12,000 people from each of the twelve tribes of Israel wear the seal of God on their foreheads. In Revelation 14:1, they are mentioned again as totaling 144,000. From these verses the Jehovah's Witnesses teach that only 144,000 people (Jehovah's Witnesses one and all) will one day go to heaven.*

Thomas covered inappropriate literal interpretation of numbers in Scripture when he addressed theories of the *chiliasts* or *millennialists* (some of whom survive today), who believe, based on a literal interpretation of Revelation 20:4-5 that references a thousand-year earthly reign of Christ before the "second resurrection" of the body at the end of the world. He notes that the number 1,000 is not to be taken literally, but denotes a great, unspecified number, as we see in Psalm 105 [104]:8: "He is mindful of his covenant forever, of the word that he commanded for a thousand generations."

Anyway, back to the issue at hand, Thomas explains that God not only *knows* in advance the number of people who will be saved (as he knows the number of grains of sand in the sea), but also *chooses* that number based on what he knows is fitting to effect the perfection of the whole of creation. It's like when a builder builds a house. He does not first pick out some certain number of stones to use; rather, he formulates the measurements of the building he envisions and determines how many stones are required. God

---

* If you'd like to know a little more about this idea, I refer you to this Q&A: "What Is the Significance of the Number 144,000 to Jehovah's Witnesses?", at https://www.catholic.com/qa/what-is-the-significance-of-the-number-144000-to-jehovahs-witnesses.

knows how many people are predestined to reside with him in heaven as is ordained for the good of the whole universe.

As to what that exact number is, only God knows! Indeed, Thomas concludes his "I answer that" section with words from the "secret" prayer in the Latin missal that reads (in translation), "To God alone is known the number for whom is reserved eternal happiness."

8 Can predestination be affected by the prayers of the saints?

Yes . . . but in a sense, the answer is both yes and no.

As regards the no, we have seen that God predestines and did so long before prayers were raised by any saints. So no, prayers of saints (our own prayers as would-be saints, or the intercessory prayers of the blessed saints in heaven) do not *cause* God to predestine anyone.

As regards the yes, predestination can be aided, helped along, or furthered by the prayers of the saints and by other good works. Predestination is part of providence, and God's providence does not rule out the efficacy of secondary causes. Salvation is predestined in such a way "that whatever helps that person toward salvation falls under the order of predestination—whether it be one's own prayers or those of another." Prayers are good works that aid in our salvation. As St. Peter tells us, "Labor the more that by good works you may make sure our calling and election" (2 Pet. 1:10).

In sum, we've got work to do to get to heaven according to God's divine plan, and that work includes prayer! Indeed, even the saints in heaven do have their work to do in aiding with our salvation: "And the smoke of the incense rose with the prayers of the saints from the hand of the angel before God" (Rev. 8:4). The saints already in heaven need no prayers for themselves. Their prayers are for us.*

Summa of God and Predestination

God . . .

1 predestines all beings, but does not predetermine of necessity rational creatures with free will.

2 is the source of predestination, and nothing inside any creature is its cause.

3 does reprobate persons to damnation who reject him through their free will.

4 does choose those who are predestined and accept his love in accordance with providence.

5 causes predestination through his grace.

6 is certain in his predestination without impairing our use of free will.

7 alone knows how many people will reside with him in heaven.

8 has arranged that the prayers of the saints and other good works can aid us in working out our predestination.

24

GOD WRITES THE BOOK OF
LIFE

The knowledge of God, by which he
firmly remembers that he has predestined some
to eternal life, is called the book of life.

ST, I, Q. 24, a. 1

Who wrote the *book of life*? He who inspired the life-giving books of the Bible, of course. It is in the books of the Bible that we learn about the "book of life." Without any lengthy preamble, Thomas simply tells us we will next consider that book.

1 Is the book of life the same as predestination?

Yes. Some were not so sure. For example, we read this in Scripture: "All these things are the book of life" (Ecclus. 24:32). A gloss says this verse references the Old and New Testaments. Therefore, the book of life is not predestination, but the Bible itself.

Thomas responds, to the contrary, that it is written: "Let them be blotted out of the book of the living" (Ps. 68:29). Further, a gloss explains: "This book is the knowledge of God, by which he hath predestined to life those whom he foreknew."

Thomas elaborates that the term "book of life" is metaphorical, comparing something in God to what we know of human affairs. When people are chosen for various public or military offices, for example, their names are recorded in a book. Consider, for example, that people are *conscripted* into the military, that word coming from the Latin *con* for "together" and *scribere*, "to write." A synonym is to *enlist* in the military (note the word *list*). Thomas says *the conscription of the predestined* is what is meant by the book of life.

As further evidence of the metaphorical use of a written book, consider that we are told of God's commandments to "write them in the tables of thy heart" (Prov. 3:3). Things are written in material books as memory aids. God needs no external aids, of course, but next we come to the quotation that started this chapter: "Whence, the knowledge of God, by which he firmly remembers that he has predestined some to eternal life, is called the book of life."

As for the objections, Thomas says that the book of life, strictly speaking, refers to "the inscription of those who are chosen to life" (i.e., predestination). But we can also speak of writing about those things that lead us to life. In this sense, the Bible itself can indeed be called "the book of life."

2 Is the book of life only about the life of glory of the predestined?

Yes, and this question is of interest for its distinction between *grace* and *glory*. One objection held that not all people who are chosen to the life of grace are chosen to the life of glory (that is, eternal life with God in heaven). Jesus said, "Have not I chosen you twelve, and one of you is a devil?" (John 6:71) when speaking of Judas. We just saw that the book of life "is the inscription of divine election," so it also applies to the life of grace. (Judas was chosen and given God's grace, yet he did not attain heaven.)

Thomas responds by reminding us that the book of life is God's knowledge of predestination. Predestination does not regard the life of grace, except as it is directed toward glory, since some people given grace fail to attain glory. The predestined attain glory, and therefore, the book of life pertains directly to glory, not grace. People are chosen with an end in mind. The soldier is chosen not merely to have his name appear on the rolls, or to put on armor, but to fight, since that is the proper act to which military service is directed. The end for which those inscribed in the book of life are meant is the life of glory.

Perhaps we could say, borrowing from St. Paul, that those who have not "fought the good fight" (2 Tim. 4:7) in God's army will not live the life of glory.

People like Judas were not written in the book of life, though they were given grace. Grace is the means God supplies to attain the end of glory. The names of those who are chosen to the life of grace but fail to attain glory are not, strictly speaking, written in the book of life. It is only in a relative sense that those with grace can be said to be written in the book of life in that they possess the means to the end, yet they may or may not attain it.

3   Can anyone get blotted out from the book of life?

Yes, unfortunately, for those who choose mortal sin over grace. One argument that led some to think otherwise built upon Augustine's statement that "God's foreknowledge, which cannot be deceived, is the book of life." Since nothing can be taken away from God's foreknowledge, nor from predestination, neither can any person's name be blotted out from the book of life.

Thomas responds again with the verse cited in this chapter's first question: "Let them be blotted out of the book of the living" (Ps. 68:29). It is quite true that God cannot be deceived or subject to change regarding his foreknowledge of the predestined, but this is not what blotting out names in the book of life entails.

Those who are ordained toward eternal life through grace, as we saw, can be said to be entered into the book of life in a relative sense, since they possess the cause or means to eternal life, but whether or not they attain that end is another matter. Those who are blotted out of the book of life are those who obtain grace but ultimately reject it through unrepented mortal sin. In a sense, through their freely chosen acts, they have wiped their own names clean from God's list.

Summa of God and the Book of Life

God is . . .

1 metaphorically speaking, the author of the book of life in which the names of the predestined are inscribed.

2 the author of the book of life, which lists only those who live the life of glory.

3 is never wrong in his foreknowledge but allows those with grace to forgo that grace if they choose, thereby erasing their names from the book of life.

25

GOD'S
POWER

All confess that God is omnipotent,
but it seems difficult to explain in what his
omnipotence precisely consists.

ST, I, Q. 25, a. 3

St. Thomas says that after considering things pertaining to the divine foreknowledge and will, it is time to consider God's power by answering six questions.

1 Does God have power?

Yes. How odd, perhaps, to think that power would not be in God, but one objection was based on Aristotle's contention that "better than every power is its act." For example, form is better than matter, form being the actualization of the potential power within matter to become some particular thing. Further, action is better than active power, since action is active power's end. Power is exercised to achieve some act. Therefore, since God, as pure act, is more perfect than power, and nothing is better than what is in God, power would be an imperfection in contrast, so there is no power in God.

Thomas first responds with Scripture: "Thou art mighty, O Lord, and thy truth is round about thee" (Ps. 88:9). He then explains that power is "twofold." There is a passive form of power in things that have the potentiality to be acted upon. Everything with *passive power* is deficient or imperfect in some way. Since we have seen that "God is pure act, simply and always perfect," there is no passive power in God.

There is also *active power*. Whereas passive power is the capacity *to be acted upon*, active power is the capacity *to act upon* something else. God possesses active power "in the highest degree."

The objection noting that act is "nobler" or better than power holds whenever act and power are distinct things. God's action is not distinct from his power, for both are his divine essence. Recall too that his existence is not distinct from his essence. Therefore, we cannot conclude there is anything in God nobler than his power.

Finally, although power, will, and knowledge differ *logically* in that power *executes* what the will *commands*, as directed *by knowledge*, in reality, the three are identified (as one) in God. We can say that God's knowledge or will as the effective principle already contains the notion of power. Hence, we considered God's knowledge and will before considering his power, "as the cause precedes the operation and effect."

2 *Is God's power infinite?*

Yes. There were some arguments to the contrary. Aristotle had written that whatever is infinite is imperfect. Since God's power is perfect, it would seem impossible that it be infinite.

Thomas replies with a quotation from St. Hilary of Poitiers: "God's power is immeasurable. He is the living mighty one." He then explains that we just saw that active power exists in God "according to the measure in which he is actual." We've seen time and again that God is pure act, and we saw too that his divine essence is infinite (Q. 7, a. 1). Therefore, the active power in God is also infinite.

For any agent that produces an effect, the more perfectly the agent possess the form by which it acts, the greater is its power to act. For example, the hotter a thing is, the greater its power to heat other things. If its own heat were infinite, it could give infinite heat. So, since God's divine essence is infinite and God acts through his essence, his power is also infinite.

As for the objection, Aristotle was referring to infinite matter not limited by form (which is therefore imperfect in that its potential has not been actualized). This does not apply to God, who, as we've seen (Q. 3, a. 2), is pure form without matter.

3 Is God omnipotent?

Yes. This might seem to follow directly from the infinitude of his power, but some cast doubt, claiming that God is not truly all-powerful because there are some things he cannot do. God cannot sin, and, as Scripture tells us, "he cannot deny himself" (2 Tim. 2:13).

Another interesting objection was based on the wording of the "collect" prayer from the Latin missal for the tenth Sunday after Pentecost, which invokes (in translation) "God who dost manifest thine almighty power chiefly in sparing and showing mercy." The objection held that surely there are things that require much greater power—"for example, to create another world." In essence, this objection posits that if God's greatest feat of power is in sparing and showing mercy, then he is not all-powerful.

Thomas responds to the contrary, "No word shall be impossible with God" (Luke 1:37).* He notes that although virtually everyone (at least in his time) agreed that God is omnipotent, the difficult part was defining just what is meant by the word *all* in saying God can do all things. He then cuts to the chase and tells us that the phrase "God can do all things" "is rightly understood to mean that God can do all things that are possible."

He elaborates with Aristotle's distinction of two ways in which a thing may be impossible. The *first way* is *in relation to a power*. Things within our human powers are possible for us (like walking), whereas things that exceed our powers are impossible for us (like flying using our bodies alone). The

---

* In the RSV-CE, this reads, perhaps more clearly, "For with God nothing will be impossible," these being the words the angel Gabriel spoke to Mary during the Annunciation.

second way is *absolute impossibility* due to the *relation in which terms* stand to each other.

Impossibility in the first way cannot apply to God. God's power infinitely exceeds human power, but to say that God is omnipotent because he can do all things possible to his power is arguing in a circle and does not really tell us anything.

God is rightly called omnipotent in the second way of considering possibility and impossibility. "God can do all things that are possible absolutely." In other words, God can do all things that are not self-contradictory and therefore absolutely impossible. God cannot make a square circle or create a boulder so massive that even he could not lift it. These things are absolutely impossible since a self-contradictory thing simply cannot exist. As Msgr. Glenn explains, "A contradictory thing is not a thing at all. It is a fiction in which two elements cancel each other and leave nothing. Thus, a square circle is a circle that is not a circle; that is to say, it is nothing whatever."[12] It is meaningless to ask if God can make such things, but their impossibility does not diminish his limitless power. Rather, they manifest God's truth, in that "a self-contradictory thing is a self-annihilating lie."

Thomas sums it up like this: "Hence it is better to say that such things cannot be done, than to say God cannot do them." (We might say that there is no "them" there to be done!) Thomas notes as well that this does not contradict Gabriel's statement, that "no word shall be impossible with God," because "whatever implies a contradiction cannot be a word, because no intellect can possibly conceive such a thing." (I know that neither of us is God, but let's try to conceive in our mind's eye just what a square circle would look like. Any luck?) Further, if we turn to the RSV-CE translation provided in our footnote and read that for God no "thing," rather than no "word," is impossible, there is no logical difference—no true, non-contradictory thing is impossible for God to do.

Let's examine the objections. That God cannot sin or deny himself does not limit his power. To sin is a failure of power, a falling short of a perfection, and God, as we've seen (Q. 7), is perfect. As to the interesting objection based on God's mercy as his greatest manifestation of power, Thomas notes that it does demonstrate God's supreme power because only he can forgive sin of his own without assistance or permission from any superior power. Further, we can say that by sparing people and showing them mercy, God leads them to participation in the infinite good in heaven, which exceeds even the creation of new worlds. We can also look upon God's divine mercy as the foundation of all of his works in creation. Nothing is due to any creature, whose existence is a gratuitous gift from God. "In this way the divine omnipotence is particularly made manifest, because to it pertains the first foundation of all good things."

4 Can God make the past not to have been?

No . . . and this one is a real doozy! (But a doozy that brings with it important clarifications of the nature of God's power.) If you enjoy science fiction, you've undoubtedly encountered stories of time travel, like H.G. Wells's *The Time Machine*. One common theme in these stories is to travel back in time to prevent some horrible event (like Hitler's rise to power). To make up a quick example, perhaps a time traveler eats a rabbit, unwittingly depriving a starving woman in the woods of food. She dies . . . and now doesn't go on to give birth to the man who was supposed to give the world some great medical discovery.

I imagine that most people would agree that we cannot travel backward in time to change things that have already happened (at least not yet!) . . . but is it truly even possible for us, or even for God almighty?

In Thomas's day, some held that God could go back in time to make events that happened not to have happened, not fully grasping the distinction between possible and impossible things. Thomas shares this profound quotation from Augustine, to the contrary: "Whoever says, if God is almighty, let him make what is done as if it were not done, does not see that this is to say, if God is almighty, let him effect that what is true, by the very fact that it is true, be false." Most intriguingly, Thomas also shares this insight from the pagan Aristotle: "Of this one thing is God alone deprived—namely, to make undone the things that have been done."

Thomas himself says, "There does not fall under the scope of God's omnipotence anything that implies a contradiction." As we saw in our last question, God is able to do all things that are non-contradictory—that is, all things that could *possibly* be done. Regarding all things possible, there are no limits to his power. He can raise the dead and create the entire universe *ex nihilo* ("out of nothing"). But because he is truth, as we saw in Q. 16, a. 5, he cannot make an event that truly happened not to have happened, which would make what was true false.

Thomas also shares an insight of great relevance to every one of us as sinners. Though even God himself cannot make it so that we had never sinned in the past, he can remove every corruption or stain of sin within our bodies and souls (recalling his limitless power of "sparing and mercy").

5   *Can God do what he does not?*

Yes. God did not *have* to make the universe we see exactly as we see it. God operates completely freely and not as necessitated by anything outside himself. In plain language, God can do whatever he wants!

Thomas begins his explanation with an intriguing quotation from God himself: "Thinkest thou that I cannot ask my Father, and he will give me presently more than twelve legions of angels?" (Matt. 26:53). Thomas points out that Jesus ended up not asking for the legions, and God the Father did not provide them, though, clearly, he could and would have had he been asked. In other words, God certainly has the power to do things that he does not do. (In fact, on an infinitely more limited scale, the same can be said for each of us.)

6   *Can God do better than what he does?*

Yes. Have you ever heard the phrase "the best of all possible worlds"? It came from the eighteenth-century philosopher Gottfried Leibniz and was repeated and parodied relentlessly in the deistic philosopher Voltaire's fantasy *Candide* as characters faced one calamity after another. This little battle of the philosophers happened about 500 years after Thomas's time, but it may have some relevance to this, our last question about God's omnipotence.

Some in Thomas's day held that God could not possibly do anything better than he does because whatever he does is done with infinite wisdom and power. Anything better would have to be done more wisely and powerfully, which cannot be, since none is wiser or more powerful than God. Though the phrase it not in the *Summa*, this objection seems to agree that the universe we see around us is, indeed, "the best of all possible worlds."

Thomas cites this powerful verse to the contrary: "God is able to do all things more abundantly than we desire or understand" (Eph. 3:20). He then elaborates on a "twofold" goodness in anything.

The *first* kind goodness of anything is related to its *essence*—for example, being rational relates to the essence of humanity. Regarding this kind of good, God can't make a thing better than what it is in itself, or it would not be the same thing, though he can make another thing that is better in some ways. Think of this in the case of numbers. God cannot make four greater than it is, "because if it were greater it would no longer be four, but another number."

The *second* kind of goodness of anything is something *over and above the essence*—for example, in man, not only to have the capacity to reason, but also to be virtuous or wise. Regarding this kind of goodness, God can indeed make better the things he has made.

"Absolutely speaking . . . God can make something else better than each thing made by him." When saying God can make a thing better that he makes it, if we take *better* as a concept *substantively*, we speak truly, because he can always make something better than each individual thing, and he can make things already made better in some respects (e.g., a more virtuous man) and not in others (e.g., making man something other than a rational being).

Now, if we take the word *better* as an *adjective* referring to the process of making things, God cannot do things better than he does them, since whatever he does is done with absolute wisdom and power. In terms of our present universe as a whole, "the present creation . . . cannot be better, on account of the most beautiful order given things by God, in which the good of the universe exists. For if any one thing were bettered, the proportion of order would be destroyed, as if one string were stretched more than it ought to be, the melody of the harp would be destroyed." Still, Thomas tells us that God could make new things and add things to the present creation that would be another and better universe.*

Summa of God's Power

God . . .

1 is powerful.

2 is infinite in his power.

3 is all-powerful (omnipotent), capable of doing all possible, non-contradictory things.

4 being truth, cannot make the past not to have been.

5 is able to do things that he does not do.

6 is able to make better things than he does, though the present universe is divinely ordered.

---

* Indeed, though he does not go into it here, Thomas elaborates on scriptural passages like Rev. 21:1—"then I saw a new heaven and a new earth"—in *ST*, Supplement, Q. 91, "Of the Quality of the World After the Judgment." (He explains, in essence, that the "best of all possible worlds" is yet to come!)

26

GOD'S DIVINE
HAPPINESS

Beatitude belongs to God in a very special manner.

ST, I, Q. 26, a. 1

Finally (for our purposes, anyway), Thomas tells us that having considered everything pertaining to the unity of God's essence, it is time to consider divine beatitude.

1 *Is God happy?*

Yes. The word *beatitude* comes from the Latin *beatitudo*, which means a state of blessedness or supreme happiness.

Thomas presents two objections that propose that beatitude does not belong to God. Boethius said that beatitude "is a state made possible by the aggregation of all good things." Aggregation is not relevant to God, who is simple and without composition. Therefore, it would seem that beatitude does not belong to God.

Further, Aristotle noted that beatitude or happiness is the reward of virtue. God receives no rewards, so it seems wrong to say he experiences beatitude.

To the contrary, Thomas, as is typical, first calls in Scripture: "Which in his times he shall show, who is the blessed and only mighty, the king of kings and lord of lords" (1 Tim. 6:15). Clearly God is "blessed," having beatitude, though Thomas explains that beatitude is in God in "a very special manner."

Thomas tells us beatitude means "the perfect good of an intellectual nature" that is able to know that it has all the good it needs and is able to control its own actions. All this applies to God in a most excellent way—namely, in that he is perfect and possesses extreme intelligence. Therefore, "beatitude belongs to God in the highest degree." There is no blessed happiness more complete than that enjoyed by God himself.

As for the first objection: there is aggregation of good in God, but in a unique manner based not on composition but on his divine simplicity. As we have seen, first in Q. 4, a. 2 on God as the source of perfections in all things, goods that are multiple and diverse in creatures pre-exist simply in the unity of God.

As for the second objection, that beatitude or happiness is the reward of virtue is an accident and not essential to virtue. It applies to human beings—who pass from potentiality to act, as we have being because of generation or reproduction—but not to God, who is pure act. As he has being, though is not begotten, he has beatitude not acquired by merit.

2 Is God called blessed in respect of his intellect?

Yes, though arguments were made that he is not. For example, beatitude is the highest good, but God is said to be good with regard to his essence, since Boethius explained that good is related to being, which is according to a thing's essence. Therefore, it seems that beatitude in God should regard his being and not his intellect.

Further, beatitude implies an end state, and the end or object of the will is good. Therefore, it seems, we should speak of God's beatitude with regard to his will, not his intellect.

Thomas first responds with a statement from Gregory the Great: "He is in glory, who while he rejoices in himself, needs not further praise." To be in glory is the same as the state of blessedness or beatitude. We enjoy God in our intellects in the *beatific vision*: as Augustine states, "Vision is the whole of the reward."* Therefore, it would seem that beatitude is also in God according to his intellect.

Thomas elaborates that, as we saw in the first question, beatitude is "the perfect good of an intellectual nature."

---

* Recall that this refers not to the sensory vision of the eye, even the eye of the glorified body in heaven, but to seeing things in the mind's eye, so to speak, through a special illumination from God (Q. 12). This manner of speaking about vision should not seem strange. After all, after understanding someone's explanation of a complicated situation or process, you've doubtless said once or twice, "Now I *see* what you're saying!"

Everything desires the perfection of its nature, and intellectual natures desire happiness as their perfection. The intellectual operation itself is the most perfect operation of an intellectual nature because, in some sense, it grasps everything. Therefore, the beatitude of an intellectual nature consists of understanding. And in God, to be and to understand are the same thing. They differ only according to our limited understanding of them.

In sum, Thomas concludes that beatitude must be assigned to God with respect to his intellect, and the same applies to the blessed (*beati*) saints and angels in heaven, by reason of how they share in God's beatitude.

As for our objections, Thomas says that Boethius's statement actually proves that beatitude is in God—not that it belongs "essentially to him under the aspect of his essence" but under the aspect of his intellect. Regarding the objection describing beatitude as an end state of satisfied desires of the will, Thomas rejoins that things desired as good by the will are first understood as good by the intellect. So, in the manner of human understanding, divine beatitude itself precedes that act whereby the will rests, having attained it. The only operation that precedes the act of will is the act of intellectual understanding, "and thus beatitude is to be found in the act of the intellect."

3 Is God the beatitude in each of the blessed in heaven?

No. Some thought that the blessed in heaven would be as happy as God himself since God is the supreme good, and the blessed will rest in him. Further, some argued, since there cannot be more than one supreme good, the beatitude of the blessed "is nothing else but God himself."

Not so, Thomas replies. As we read in a metaphorical passage from Scripture, "Star differeth from star in glory" (1 Cor. 15:41). This means that the beatitude some experience in heaven will be greater than that experienced by others.

If we look at beatitude only from the perspective of its *object*, then yes, God is the only supreme good and the only beatitude. Indeed, as Augustine has stated so beautifully, "Blessed is he who knoweth thee, though he know nought else." Still, regarding the *act* of understanding, there can be multiple degrees of beatitude within created beings. (Perhaps you will recall from our discussion of Q. 12, a. 6 that those with the greatest charity, who love God most deeply, will see his essence most clearly.)

Thus, we see, contrary to our objections, that first, whereas the *object* of beatitude is supreme good absolutely, in the *acts* of understanding within creatures, some can participate in that good more fully than others. Second, regarding ends, Aristotle reminds us that we must also consider *objective* and *subjective* ends—"namely, the *thing itself* and its *use*." A miser's end is money and its acquisition. In a similar manner, God is the *objective* last end, "the thing itself" at which every rational creature aims, whereas created beatitude is the *subjective* end—"the use, or rather fruition, of the thing."

In simple terms, the degree to which we accept and reciprocate God's love on earth will determine how fully we will be able to enjoy him—with *enjoyment* being the fruition of our charity in beatitude and *him* being the ultimate "thing itself" in heaven.

4 *Is all other beatitude included in the beatitude of God?*

Yes. Some thought otherwise because there are "false beatitudes," like sensual pleasures, riches, and so forth, but there is no falsity in God, and God is not corporeal but spirit.

Thomas responds that beatitude is a perfection, and we saw way back in Q. 4, a. 2 that the divine perfection "embraces all other perfections. . . . Therefore, the divine beatitude embraces all other perfections."

As for all the "false" or limited beatitudes people might seek on earth, God possesses every true beatitude in the most eminent degree, since all goods pre-exist in him. God enjoys the ultimate *contemplative* happiness in contemplating himself and all things of creation, and as regards *active* operations, God governs the entire universe. Whereas those of us on earth may seek happiness through things like wealth, power, dignity, and fame (as Boethius has pointed out), God possesses himself and all other things for his delight. Instead of wealth, God is completely self-sufficient, which is the goal of the accumulation of riches. Instead of power, he has omnipotence. Instead of dignities, God is the ruler of all things. Instead of fame, God has "the admiration of all creatures."

As for false beatitudes, they are called false because they fall short in various ways of true happiness. Therefore, they do not exist in God. Still, to the extent that they have some semblance of true beatitude, this we find first pre-existing in the divine beatitude. Finally, the good that exists in material things also exists in God "but in a spiritual manner."

Thomas ends abruptly: "We have now spoken enough concerning what pertains to the unity of the divine essence."

If enough is enough for Thomas, then enough is enough for us.

Summa of God's Divine Happiness

God . . .

1 enjoys the infinite happiness of divine beatitude.

2 enjoys beatitude in his divine intellect in unity with his divine essence.

3 has ordered the universe so that some of the blessed will experience greater beatitude than others.

4 in his perfect beatitude, embraces all forms of beatitude.

Conclusion

WHO
IS GOD?

Having considered what belongs to the unity
of the divine essence, it remains to treat of what
belongs to the Trinity of the persons in God.

ST, I, Q. 27, Prologue

After considering the last end of human life,
and the virtues and vices, there should follow the
consideration of the Savior of all, and of
the benefits bestowed by him on the human race.

ST, III, Prologue

We have seen how the young boy Thomas's question—"What is God?"—spurred him to produce an astounding array of the most sublime answers through the next forty-four years of his life on earth back in the thirteenth century.

Modern researchers have investigated how the understanding of God tends to grow and mature within ordinary people in our day as *we* progress from children into mature adults. Theologian James Fowler, for example, produced an empirical, evidence-based theory of the stages of faith development. In *Stages of Faith*[13] and in other writings, he detailed his findings based on interviews with individuals from age three to eighty-four. He found that as we mature and develop, from early childhood toward the end of life, there is a common and predictable course of increasing abstraction and sophistication in faith that parallels growth in cognitive abilities (demonstrated by psychologist Jean Piaget) and growth in moral development (documented by psychologist Lawrence Kohlberg).

Fowler and his associates found that through the early and later childhood years, during stages they called *intuitive-projective* and *mythic-literal faith*, we commonly find simple and concrete beliefs. Here we may find God as that kindly old bearded Father, resting upon his cloud.

By the time we reach adolescence, and our abilities to think abstractly have blossomed, we see *synthetic-conventional* faith, in which religious beliefs become organized and synthesized into coherent systems, usually meshing with those of our family or influential peers.

In early adulthood, some individuals will begin to question and think deeply about their religious beliefs during the stage of *individuative-reflective* faith. This is especially common when they have encountered life experiences that challenge their beliefs (perhaps in their college courses). As they search for a belief system that makes sense to them, they may reject some or all of their prior beliefs, as happened to me, and so many young people today, who class themselves as atheists or agnostics or "nones," having no religious affiliation.

Some people will experience the stage of *conjunctive* faith in middle age, in which understanding deepens—for example, the capacity to make sense of paradoxes, such as the existence of suffering when God is all loving (a topic we've come across more than once in these pages!).

Finally, a rare few may attain the highest stage of *universalizing* faith, in which we achieve a sense of oneness with being and of universal love. One of the modern-day examples that Fowler (a Methodist minister) provided was Mother Teresa of Calcutta.

I wonder if any of these descriptions has rung any bells for you. Perhaps you can say "been there, done that" for some of Fowler's stages. And who would not love to join St. Teresa in embracing and enjoying *universalizing* faith?

How would our Angelic Doctor have scored on such a test of faith? Key components for growth in faith, according to Fowler, include developing cognitive powers and abstract thinking abilities. Thomas knew such thinking powers well, having written, "Experience shows that some understand more profoundly than do others, as one who carries a conclusion to its first principles and ultimate causes understands it better than one who reduces it to its proximate causes" (*ST,* I, Q. 85, a. 7). Indeed, who on earth would come to a more profound understanding of first principles and *the* ultimate cause of all than Thomas Aquinas?

Yet as awesome and profound as is the Prime Mover, First Cause, Necessary Being, Thomas knew well that God is so much more than any mere abstraction from reality. Rather, God is reality itself. Thomas was well aware that the so-called "god of the philosophers," the god reason can show us to exist, is also the great "I Am" of Scripture, and the "god of Abraham, Isaac, and Jacob" (Exod. 3:14-15). Thomas did not only ask, "*What* is God?" He asked, "*Who* is God?" as well.

Who is God?

Here at the end of Thomas's twenty-six questions on the existence and nature of God in the unity of his divine essence, we have reached only page 143 of the *Summa Theologica* in the English-only translation I use (albeit in rather small double-columned print). That leaves us with 2,868 pages to go!

Recall that theology is the "sacred science" of the study of God. Thomas has plenty left to say about God and all that flows from him. In the questions we examined, we saw that God is referred to as a *person*, and we saw references from Scripture now and again to God the Father, the Son, and the Holy Spirit, but only to elucidate our examination of God "in the unity of his essence."

Yet in the next question, number 27, "The Procession of the Divine Persons," Thomas properly begins to examine the overarching question of not only *what* but *who* God is. (This chapter's opening quotation provides Thomas's opening words.)

Thomas's analysis of the divine persons, he tells us, is based on what God has revealed to us about himself, being inaccessible to human reason alone, but which reason can help us better to understand. Here Thomas examines how the God who is *one* in his *essence* is also *three persons*. He devotes a full seventeen questions, with dozens of articles, to the Holy Trinity.

Far from finished yet, it is in the third part of the great *Summa Theologica*, in the "Treatise on the Incarnation," that we meet God made man, the Word made flesh, in the person of the Son of God, our Lord and Savior, Jesus Christ. Indeed, though Christ is addressed in the third of three parts of the *Summa*, he is placed there to complete the great circle of God: God's outflowing creation, including man, and Christ as man's means to return to God. Thomas explains what it means to say that Christ is both the alpha and the omega, the beginning and the end, both the way and the destination, and so much more over the course of over 300 pages.

The question "Who is God?" cannot be answered in any length in this book. Those who care to find out what the Angelic Doctor said are guided to *ST*, I, Qs. 27-43 on the Trinity and III, Qs. 1-59 on the Incarnation.

Though Thomas understood the essence and attributes of God in a depth that few before or after him ever had or would, he never forgot that God is love. He had what we might call today a most intimate "personal relationship with Jesus Christ." It is reported that not long before Thomas's death, Christ appeared to him in a mystical vision. He told Thomas he had written well about him, and he asked what Thomas might want from him. Thomas replied, "*Non nisi te Domine*"—nothing but you, Lord.

Surely, through the fires of charity that burned in his heart and inflamed his intellect, since his death on March 7, 1274, St. Thomas Aquinas has received his answers as to what and who God is, as he basks in the beatific vision, beholding the loving God to whom he had devoted all.

May St. Thomas inspire us all to see God more clearly, love him more dearly, and follow him more nearly, day by day,* until the day we see him face to face and know him as he is.

---

* Adapting a bit the beautiful prayer of St. Richard of Chichester.

APPENDIX A

Attributes of God as Classified by John of St. Thomas

In this first treatise, where God is considered
in the unity of his nature, one should notice
the profundity with which St. Thomas orders
and classifies the divine attributes.

John of St. Thomas[14]

The seventeenth-century Portuguese philosopher and theologian João Poinsot (1589-1654) was so devoted to the wisdom of St. Thomas Aquinas that when he professed as a Dominican, he took the name he is best known by to this day: John of St. Thomas (*John* being the anglicized version of *João*). After thirty years as a renowned professor in Spain, he remarked near the end of his life that he had never taught or written a word contrary to the teachings of Thomas Aquinas.

John may have inherited Thomas's gentle and saintly demeanor as well as his intellect. Though he was an astute theological disputant, biographers report that he never once hurt the feelings of an opponent in discussion! (How many modern debaters could say the same?)

I have found John of St. Thomas of great help. His book *The Seven Gifts of the Holy Ghost* helped me explain his and Thomas's insights in my own *Seven Gifts of the Holy Spirit*.

Of interest here, though, is another of our good Portuguese Dominican's works, *An Introduction to the Summa Theologiae of St. Thomas Aquinas.*

In his analysis of the divine attributes, John describes five of them as "primordial entitative attributes of God" and as "radical attributes pertaining to the very existence" that "remove from the notion of pure act as uncreated being."[15] By that he meant that these fundamental attributes logically flow from this notion, and by using the word "remove," he means they logically follow from five defects found in all created and potential being: "composition, imperfection, limitation, change, and division or plurality." When we "remove" these conditions, we are employing the negative theology Thomas used, since the Latin *remotio* means a taking away or negation. Removing from composition, we obtain simplicity; from imperfection, we obtain perfection; from limitation, infinity; from change, immutability; and from division or plurality, unity.

John of St. Thomas is simply providing us with a summary of what his namesake already did, as we have seen. We might think of it as a primer to help us understand and remember it.

Attributes of Potential Beings	Attributes of Pure Act
Composition	Simplicity
Imperfection	Perfection
Limitation	Infinity
Change	Immutability
Division or Plurality	Unity

John notes as well that three "secondary entitative attributes" follow logically from God's five "primordial entitative attributes." To summarize John, who is summarizing Thomas, let's take another look at these attributes in brief.

Goodness: God's supreme goodness follows from his *perfection*. Goods are that we desire, and God is the ultimate cause and fulfillment of our desires. All goodness in created things comes from God. Whereas created things *possess* goodness, God *is* goodness itself.

Immensity: God's immensity follows from his *infinity* and refers to his omnipresence—the fact that he is everywhere. Scripture tells us so: "It is written, 'I fill heaven and earth'" (Jer. 23:24). As we saw before, reason tells us God is in every thing in three ways:

A through his *essence* because he causes and sustains all things,

B through his *presence* because he sees and knows all things, and

C through his *power* because all things are subject to his rule.

Eternity: God's eternity follows from his *immutability*. Since God is unchangeable, he is not limited by time and can have no beginning or end, but partakes of eternity: "The simultaneously whole and perfect possession of interminable life."[16]

Here, for review and edification, are the five primary and three secondary attributes of God as classified by John of St. Thomas (with secondary attributes listed beside the primary attributes from which they flow).

Primordial Entitative Attributes	Secondary Entitative Attributes
Simplicity	
Perfection	Goodness
Infinity	Immensity
Immutability	Eternity
Unity	

All of these attributes are addressed in the first eleven questions of Thomas's *Summa Theologica* and in the first eleven chapters of this book. John of St. Thomas also provides further analysis of the remaining fifteen questions of Thomas's Treatise on God (*ST,* I, Qs. 12–26), but, to borrow previously cited words from Thomas, "we have now spoken enough concerning what pertains to the unity of the divine essence." Readers who care to see John of St. Thomas's full treatment are directed to the text of his *Introduction to the Summa Theologiae of Thomas Aquinas.*

APPENDIX B

God Is . . . Master Summary List

A disposition becomes a habit,
just as a boy becomes a man.

ST, I-II, Q. 49, a. 2

Finally, dear reader, I ask if you recall from way back in our introduction that another great Dominican saint, Rose of Lima, once asked her confessor for a list of 150 of God's divine perfections so that she might meditate on them in prayer. Well, I've taken the liberty to glean a total of 133 conclusions that the grown-up Thomas provided in answer to his famous burning childhood question: "What is God?"

I have culled these from the summaries that appeared at the end of most of our chapters but cast them all into statements starting with "God is." Hopefully, they will provide you with things to meditate upon, wonder about, and pray to the God who is!

Thomas the Boy: What is God?

Thomas the Man:

1   God is *not* self-evident to man.

2   God is provable by reason to exist, starting simply with evidence of the senses.

3   God is the prime or unmoved mover. (First way— argument from motion or change.)

4   God is the uncaused cause. (Second way—argument from cause and effect.)

5   God is the only necessary being. (Third way— argument from necessary being.)

6   God is the perfection of being. (Fourth way— argument from the perfection of being.)

7   God is final cause of all that exists. (Fifth way— argument from divine governance.)

8   God is pure spirit.

9   God is pure form.

10   God is the same as his essence or nature.

11   God is his own essence and existence.

12   God is utterly unique and beyond genus (or classification).

13   God is pure act (completely actualized substance).

14   God is absolutely primal being.

15   God is completely perfect.

16   God is the source of perfection in created beings.

17   God is the first and universal principle of being.

18 God is good.

19 God is the supreme good and most excellent cause of all good.

20 God is the only being whose essence or nature is good itself.

21 God is the source and donor of every good that exists in any creature as its own.

22 God is infinite, limitless, without beginning or end.

23 God is alone absolute, actual infinity as self-subsistent being.

24 God is infinite as self-subsistent spirit without measurable quantity.

25 God is alone in absolute, actual infinity, unlike any potential infinities of multitude.

26 God is in all things.

27 God is in all places.

28 God is everywhere by his essence, presence, and power.

29 God is the only omnipresent being.

30 God is completely immutable or unchangeable (in that he is pure act).

31 God is unique in immutability.

32 God is eternal.

33 God is the only eternal being.

34 God is not limited by time.

35 God is beyond aeviternity.

36 God is one.

37 God is uniquely and supremely one.

38 God is seen in his essence by the blessed in heaven.

39 God is not seen in his essence through images or similitudes.

40 God is not seen in his essence with the bodily eye.

41 God is not seen in his essence by any natural power.

42 God is seen in his essence by the light of illumination or glory.

43 God is seen in his essence most clearly by those who love him the most.

44 God is such that what is seen is through his essence and not through a creature's images.

45 God is such that creatures see all things when they see things in his essence or Word.

46 God is impossible for living creatures to see in his essence, except through a miracle.

47 God is knowable by natural reason in *that* he exists, but not in *what* his essence is.

48 God is knowable in a way that transcends natural reason through his supernatural grace.

49 God is nameable by his creatures.

50 God is named in his substance, as good, wise, etc., in an imperfect way.

51 God is namable in the literal sense, as in words like *being*, *good*, *living*, and others.

52 God is rightly given multiple names that are not synonymous or redundant.

53 God is named analogously by names citing multiple perfections in creatures that are one in him.

54 God is known through creatures, but the names apply primarily to him.

55 God is properly given some temporal (time-based) names like *Creator*, *Lord*, and *Savior*.

56 God is named *God* according to his divine providence over all things.

57 God is the name of God alone and cannot be shared by any other.

58 God is named truly by Catholics, but not by unbelievers who don't know his nature.

59 God is most properly named "*He Who Is*," as he gave his name to Moses.

60 God is nameable through affirmative statements, not only through negation.

61 God is holder of the highest place in knowledge of all things.

62 God is able to understand himself.

63 God is able to comprehend himself.

64 God is one in that his intellect is his substance or essence.

65 God is able to know all things outside himself.

66 God is able to know all things with proper, particular knowledge.

67 God is able to know all things at once.

68 God is the cause of things through his knowledge.

69 God is aware even of things that are not, but exist only in potentiality.

70 God is aware of evil things.

71 God is aware of singular, individual things (like you and me).

72 God is aware of even infinite things.

73 God is aware of even future, possible things like voluntary acts of the human will.

74 God is aware of enunciable things humans express in language.

75 God is as unchangeable in his knowledge as he is in his essence.

76 God is able to comprehend both practical and speculative knowledge of all things.

77 God is possessor of many ideas, as ideas of all things flow from his knowledge of his essence.

78 God is possessor of ideas of all creatable things as exemplars and all knowable things as types.

79 God is possessor of truth completely and simply, rather than through any reasoning process.

80 God is truth itself.

81 God is possessor of the one primary truth, possessed as many within many created intellects.

82 God is possessor of eternal truth within his divine intellect.

83 God is unchangeable in his truth.

84 God is without any falsity, which is possible only in the fallible judgment of created intellects.

85 God is alive, as are any self-moving beings with souls.

86 God is alive in his essence, and not merely through operations.

87 God is possessor of life in the highest degree, perfect and eternal.

88 God is life, as he is knowledge, in his divine simplicity.

89 God is possessor of a will.

90 God is willer of his own goodness, and he wills that creatures share in that goodness.

91 God is such that he wills only his own good necessarily.

92 God is the cause of things through his will.

93 God is uncaused in his will, as his will and intellect are one.

94 God is never without fulfillment of his will, but we must distinguish between what he wills antecedently and consequently.

95 God is possessor of an unchangeable will that permits creatures to change.

96 God is the imposer of necessity on some things, but he allows other things to act on their own wills.

97 God is not responsible for evil through actively willing it, though he permits it so greater good may arise.

98 God is possessor of free will for all things except that he, of necessity, wills his own goodness (as per #91).

99 God is willing to make his will known through a variety of expressions.

100 God is expressive of his will by prohibitions, precepts, counsel, operations, and permission.

101 God is love, as he is will, love being the first movement of will.

102 God is in love with all things, and his love causes them to exist.

103 God is in love with some things more than others.

104 God is in love with better things more than with lesser things.

105 God is just, distributing to all things perfections in due proportion.

106 God is both justice and truth, in will and in intellect.

107 God is merciful, remedying defects in all created things, in fulfillment of justice.

108 God is both just and merciful in all of his works.

109 God is providential, overseeing, caring for, guiding, and governing all of creation.

110 God is governor and protector of every single being, though he exercises his providence in different ways to different creatures, according to their natures.

111 God is the primary cause of every single being in its nature, but he grants creatures the power of secondary causation to aid in governing the universe.

112 God is the giver of free will to human beings, and his divine providence does not prevent us from guiding our own actions by our own free choices.

113 God is the cause of predestination, but he does not predetermine the acts of rational beings.

114 God is the source of predestination, not anything inside any creatures.

115 God is permissive of the reprobation (damnation) of those who choose to reject him.

116 God is active in choosing those who are predestined and accepting of his love.

117 God is the cause of predestination through his grace.

118 God is certain in his predestination without hindering the use of our free will.

119 God is alone in the knowledge of how many people will spend eternity with him in heaven.

120 God is generous in sharing his power so that secondary causes, like the prayers of the saints, can help us get to heaven.

121 God is, metaphorically speaking, the author of the book of life.

122 God is the author of the book of the life, which lists those who live the life of glory.

123 God is the author of the book of life, from which people may choose to blot out their names.

124 God is powerful.

125 God is infinite in his power.

126 God is omnipotent, all-powerful, to do all possible, non-contradictory things.

127 God is truth and, therefore, cannot make the past not to have been.

128 God is able to do things he does not do.

129 God is able to do better things than he does, and a new heaven and earth await us.

130 God is infinitely happy in his eternal beatitude.

131 God is happy in his intellect, which is one with his essence.

132 God is dispenser of varying degrees of beatitude to creatures depending on how deeply they share in his love while on earth.

133 God is happy in a way that embraces, pre-exists, and produces all other forms of beatitude.

Sit laus Deo in sempiternum!*

---

* Praise be to God forever!

ABOUT THE AUTHOR

Kevin Vost holds a doctorate degree in psychology and has taught psychology at Aquinas College in Nashville, the University of Illinois at Springfield, MacMurray College, and Lincoln Land Community College. He has served as a research review committee member for American Mensa, a society promoting the scientific study of human intelligence. Kevin is a prolific writer, having written more than twenty books, including Catholic Answers' *Memorize the Reasons!*, and he appears regularly in Catholic media.

ENDNOTES

1 Marcus Aurelius, *Meditations*, bk. 4, ch. 3, 6.24, 7.17, 8.17, 9.28, 9.39, 10.6, 12.14, 12.24.

2 Seneca, *Epistles 1-65*, Richard Gummere, trans. (Cambridge, MA: Harvard University Press, 2006), 273 (Epistle 41).

3 *Epictetus: Discourses Books I-II*, trans. W.A. Oldfather (Cambridge, MA: Harvard University Press, 2000), p. 111 (*Discourse* I.16, Translation first published in 1928).

4 Brian Davies, *Thomas Aquinas' Summa Theologiae: A Guide & Commentary* (New York, NY: Oxford University Press, 2014), p. 54.

5 Msgr. Paul J. Glenn, *A Tour of the Summa: A Journey Through St. Thomas Aquinas' Summa Theologiae* (Rockford, IL: TAN Books, 1978), p. 9.

6 Ibid., p. 10.

7 St. Thomas Aquinas, *Commentary on the Book of Job*, Brian Beckett Mullady, O.P., STD, trans. (Lander, Wyoming: The Aquinas Institute for the Study of Sacred Doctrine, 2016), p. 248.

8 "Eternal-now" definition, YourDictionary.com, https://www.your dictionary.com/eternal-now.

9 Michael Lipka, "10 Facts About Atheists" (Pew Research Center, Dec. 6, 2019). https://www.pewresearch.org/fact-tank/2019/12/06/10-facts-about-atheists.

10 St. Thomas Aquinas, *The Aquinas Catechism: A Simple Explanation of the Catholic Faith by the Church's Greatest Theologian*, Ralph McInerney, trans. (Manchester, NH: Sophia Institute Press, 2000), p. 130.

11 Glenn, p. 25.

12 Ibid., p. 26.

13 James W. Fowler, *Stages of Faith: The Psychology of Human Development* (New York: HarperOne, 1995).

14 John of St. Thomas, *Introduction to the Summa Theologiae of St. Thomas Aquinas*, trans. Ralph McInerny (South Bend, IN: St. Augustine's Press, 2004), p. 25.

15 Ibid., p. 27.

16 *ST*, I, Q. 10, a. 1, citing Boethius, *De Consol. V: On the Consolation of Philosophy*, bk. 5.